Gold EXPERIENCE

B2

First for Schools

Workbook
Skills
Grammar
Vocabulary

Mary Stephens

Contents

READING

1 Read the interviews and choose the correct answer, true or false.

1 Sophie is currently studying art.
   True   <u>False</u>

2 Sophie has already made money from her music.
   True   False

3 Jason is a singer-songwriter.
   True   False

4 Jason never gets nervous.
   True   False

5 This is Zoe's first audition.
   True   False

6 Zoe is a student at the moment.
   True   False

7 Paul doesn't care what the judges think of him.
   True   False

8 Paul claims he isn't what he seems.
   True   False

2 Read the interviews again. Match the contestants (A–D) with the sentences (1–10).

1 __D__ tries to get people to reconsider their ideas.

2 _____ mentions that they write musical compositions.

3 _____ hasn't managed to pass auditions previously.

4 _____ is ready to behave better than normally tonight.

5 _____ has abandoned the chance to study because of this show.

6 _____ is worried about how the show may affect their reputation.

7 _____ believes their other skills may give them an advantage.

8 _____ is postponing their studies for a time.

9 _____ doesn't think they'll get too frightened to think.

10 _____ expresses surprise at their recent success.

Reaching for the Stars!

They got through last week's auditions. Meet tonight's Star Talent contestants, Sophie, Jason, Zoe and Paul!

A Sophie

I've been singing and playing the guitar for some time now. I started off in a band but it didn't work out – in fact it put me off the whole idea for a while. After we split up, I enrolled at art college. I'm very creative so I loved it: brush, stencils, spray can – you name it, I've painted with it! I've taken a break for now but I'll go back to it again one day. I didn't do any gigs during that time but I did some busking – which is how I got hooked on the music business all over again! I wasn't sure about auditioning for this show. I watched it last year and, without wanting to hurt anyone's feelings, I found some of the contestants weird! I'm quite cool – a bit of a trendsetter and I don't want to be identified with anything second-rate. But there's a record contract waiting for the winner so I'd be a fool not to give it a try.

B Jason

Singing is my passion – I've given up a place at business college to follow my dream. I've been wanting to get up on stage and perform for as long as I remember. I'm doing a cover song for the show this week, but to my own arrangement. I'm hoping to sing some of my own material next time round – provided I get through tonight of course. I sometimes find it hard to express my feelings so I do it through my songs. We're performing to a huge studio audience tonight, which is very scary, but I can't give up now. Last week's auditions were really nerve-wracking too, but getting through them improved my self-confidence a lot. I'm pretty level-headed normally and I don't tend to panic. Let's hope it's the same tonight! If I get the performance right, the rest shouldn't matter anyway.

C Zoe

I've always loved singing and dancing – I'm addicted to it! I'd really love a career in music so I go to as many auditions as I can. It knocks my confidence when I get turned down but I'm determined so I try not to let that worry me. I'm coming to the end of my university course luckily – choosing between being a household name and getting a degree could have been a hard decision! You need plenty of self-confidence to do this – if you hang back or let your nerves take over you don't stand a chance of getting through. Of course you don't want to look like a show-off either – that would really put the judges off. I think the experience I've gained from studying drama will come in useful tonight and help me stand out from the crowd. I hope so, anyway!

D Paul

I can't believe I've got through to the live show tonight. I know at least one of the judges at last week's audition found me outspoken and a bit too laid back ... but that's just how I am. I've always been a rebel – my tutors tried to make me conform and then kicked me out of college when I refused. I'm not going to waste this chance though – winning could change my life. So if I have to act like I'm a saint to impress the judges, that's what I'll do. My friends have suggested I hide my tattoos and piercings for the performance but if you're a rebel like me you want to challenge people's assumptions. If the judges look deep enough, they'll find I value qualities like loyalty and generosity as much as they do, in myself as well as in others.

VOCABULARY
Hanging out

1 Find ten personality adjectives. The words go across, down or diagonally. The first letter of each word is highlighted.

m	i	t	a	s	p	a	y	n	e	l	l	o	r	t
z	p	b	e	o	q	r	x	s	p	o	i	l	e	d
p	n	l	j	c	o	c	a	r	i	n	g	k	k	n
n	n	m	o	i	m	o	v	x	l	o	o	n	p	h
n	o	i	t	a	d	u	a	m	z	w	u	x	t	q
c	o	t	p	b	p	j	n	g	x	u	t	s	b	q
g	e	g	i	l	x	r	v	e	v	m	s	h	o	d
h	y	t	u	e	o	q	v	l	x	o	p	y	s	q
o	p	g	a	b	d	r	j	e	r	o	o	a	s	j
m	h	f	b	h	e	u	i	b	f	d	k	y	y	o
a	j	u	d	w	e	g	o	r	u	y	e	w	z	b
s	t	l	l	v	n	c	t	i	s	r	n	v	l	l
s	h	t	h	x	c	o	w	t	s	e	z	k	g	p
v	v	o	e	x	f	o	o	y	y	f	w	f	d	u
p	k	l	p	n	l	l	u	n	c	e	b	i	o	g

2 Put the word in brackets in the correct place in the sentence.

1 We all wanted to win the race, but we couldn't keep _____up_____ with the leader. (up)

2 Skateboarding didn't use to be my thing, but I'm really _____ it now! (into)

3 Nothing will ever put me _____ dancing; I love it too much. (off)

4 I don't like drama lessons, so I'm planning to give them _____ next term. (up)

5 You'll never stop Sonya from watching TV; she's completely addicted _____ it. (to)

6 If I were better _____ the guitar, I could join my friend's band. (at)

3 Put the words in order to make correct sentences.

1 was / plain / a / boring / He / a / black / wearing / tracksuit / .
   He was wearing a boring plain black tracksuit.

2 a / dress / dressed / in / flowery / knee-length / pink / She / was / .
   _____

3 baggy / relaxed / grey / in / comfortable / He / pants / .
   _____

4 dress / wore / She / short / a / stunning / woollen / .
   _____

5 in / amazing / a / blue / was / She / T-shirt / really / dressed / .
   _____

6 a / cotton / He / hoodie / navy / trendy / was / wearing / .
   _____

7 a / actress / beautiful / dress / silk / The / white / wore / .
   _____

8 blue / I / jeans / like / tight / wearing / denim / .
   _____

4 Complete the sentences with an appropriate word.

1 I'm sorry! I didn't mean to _____hurt_____ your feelings.

2 Zara has become a celebrity, but I'm sure she'll keep her _____ on the ground.

3 Relax – don't _____ life so seriously!

4 At weekends, I enjoy hanging _____ with my friends.

5 To get noticed, you need to _____ out from the crowd.

6 Failing the audition really knocked his _____ .

7 I'm very independent, so I like doing my _____ thing.

8 That singer's so famous he's become a household _____ .

9 I don't like classical ballet much, but I'm really _____ hip-hop.

10 Tom worries about everything, but his brother is much more laid- _____ .

GRAMMAR
Present and present perfect tenses

1 Complete the table and then complete the sentences below.

	Infinitive	Past simple	Past participle
1	buy	bought	*bought*
2	fall	fell	
3	know	knew	
4	meet	met	
5	sing	sang	
6	steal	stole	

a My parents *have bought* me a brilliant computer game for my birthday!

b Oh no! Someone .... my MP3 player!

c .... you .... Robert's new girlfriend yet?

d I .... out with my neighbour. We never speak to each other nowadays.

e My brother .... with some of the most famous bands in our country; he's playing in our town next week.

f I .... Emma for long, but she's definitely my best friend now.

2 Put the words in the correct order.

1 instead of studying / playing / always / My brother / computer games / is / .
My brother is always playing computer games instead of studying.

2 seen / that clip / I / have / on / before / YouTube / never / .

3 wanted / to be / She / always / an actress / has / .

4 living / for ten years / have / here / been / We / .

5 have / How long / drama / studying / you / been?

6 arranged / in the park / We / just / have / to meet / .

7 yet / that dance / learnt / you / Have?

8 has been / March / a video / Our class / since / making / .

3 Choose the correct answer, A, B or C.

1 I can't come out because I .... my homework.
  A am doing
  B do
  C have done

2 My brother annoys me because he ....
  A is never listening
  B never listens
  C never is listening

3 How many texts .... so far today?
  A have you sent
  B did you send
  C are you sending

4 I .... to be famous.
  A have never been wanting
  B am never wanting
  C have never wanted

5 I'm sweating because I ....
  A have jogged
  B am being jogging
  C have been jogging

6 Can you play the guitar well? No, I .... to learn it.
  A have just started
  B have just been starting
  C just have started

7 Sorry I'm late! How long .... ?
  A are you waiting
  B have you been waiting
  C have you waited

8 .... acting?
  A Have you always been loving
  B Are you always loving
  C Have you always loved

4 Choose the correct verb form.

1 *I've finished/I've been finishing/I finish* the book now so you can have it if you like.

2 How many slices of pizza *are you eating/have you eaten/have you been eating* so far?

3 She hasn't slept because *she's travelled/she travels/she's been travelling.*

4 Emma's really annoying – she *always is bossing/is always bossing/bosses always* my friends around.

5 How long *have you known/are you knowing/have you been knowing* your best friend?

6 When *I'm not studying/I haven't studied/I don't study,* I hang out with my friends.

USE OF ENGLISH
Vocabulary: collocations

1 Choose the correct answer, A, B or C.

1 Clare and I are _____ mates; we always go everywhere together.
   A top   (B) best   C first

2 My brother loves rock bands and I hate them, so we're total _____ when it comes to music.
   A opposites   B differences   C contrasts

3 Some brothers and sisters fight because of sibling _____.
   A disagreement   B enmity   C rivalry

4 My penfriend and I are a perfect match because we have _____ interests.
   A same   B common   C equal

5 Sometimes I could murder my sister, other times I adore her; we have a real love-hate _____.
   A relationship   B friendship   C partnership

6 Since Laura stole her friend's boyfriend they've been _____ enemies.
   A born   B torn   C sworn

7 Jason is one of my _____ friends and I'd trust him with my life!
   A nearest   B closest   C hardest

2 Complete the text with the best answer, A, B, C or D.

Who needs friends?

We all need friends to hang 1) _out_ with. A really good friend is someone 2) _____ can share your secrets with and who is on your side when life gets tough. Most best mates have 3) _____ interests; they think the same and enjoy the same things you 4) _____.
Of course, friendships between 5) _____ opposites are possible too, but these are less common. Remember that friends can disagree and even your 6) _____ friend may drive you crazy from time to time. If you're really unlucky, a friend can end up being your sworn 7) _____, especially if they 'steal' your boyfriend or girlfriend! Even if you have a loyal best friend it's important that you keep 8) _____ new friends – if you always hang out with just one person, you'll forget how to socialise with other people and you'll end up being extremely boring yourself!

1 **A** up   **B** in   **C** out   **D** down
2 **A** they   **B** who   **C** that   **D** you
3 **A** equal   **B** common   **C** decided **D** same
4 **A** are   **B** have   **C** do   **D** too
5 **A** complete **B** decided **C** whole   **D** great
6 **A** oldest   **B** grandest **C** finest   **D** largest
7 **A** rivalry   **B** opposite **C** competitor **D** enemy
8 **A** forming   **B** making   **C** doing   **D** having

3 Complete the sentences with the correct form of the word in capitals.

1 I'm no longer on _speaking_ terms with my mum!   SPEAK

2 Clare is very _____ so I imagine she'll end up as an artist or a sculptor.   CREATE

3 That boy changes his girlfriend every week – he's got no idea of _____ at all!   LOYAL

4 Thanks to my grandad's _____, I've got enough money to buy a car!   GENEROUS

5 Sandra isn't very pretty, but her sister's extremely _____.   BEAUTY

6 Being _____ and ordering people about is never going to make you popular!   BOSS

7 There's a lot of _____ between my sister and I.   RIVAL

8 Have you got a good _____ with your parents?   RELATION

9 She and her ex-boyfriend are _____ enemies!   SWEAR

10 One day, I would like to be rich and _____.   SUCCEED

4 Complete the words in the sentences.

1 My sister is very ungrateful; she takes everything for gr _a_ _n_ _t_ ed.

2 Laura stole Emma's boyfriend, which destroyed their r _____ a _____ p.

3 Tom's completely ob _____ d with dancing; he thinks of nothing else.

4 George is a tr _____ tt _____; all his friends try to copy his clothes and his behaviour.

5 My friend is a complete r _____ and opposes everyone in authority!

6 My brother goes to lots of auditions, but all he gets are r ____ j _____ on ____.

7 She's always so s _____ b _____ n! She refuses to change her mind no matter how you try to persuade her.

8 My little brother is completely s _____ d; my parents give him everything he wants.

USE OF ENGLISH
Grammar: present perfect or past simple?

1 Put the verbs in brackets into the correct tense, present perfect or past simple.

1 We _formed_ our rock band about a year ago. (form)
2 He's tired because he _____ a long way. (run).
3 I _____ anyone when I arrived at the party. (not/recognise)
4 I'm worried about Barry because he _____ me for ages. (not/text)
5 They _____ abroad for two years before moving here. (live)
6 When _____ school? (she/leave)
7 Why _____ Paul _____ anyone that he'd finished with his girlfriend? (not/tell)
8 Sarah _____ a great video from YouTube the other day. (download)
9 Oh no, I _____ my phone! (lose)
10 For my last birthday, my parents _____ for me to learn the guitar. (pay)

2 Rewrite the sentences so they have a similar meaning. Use the word in brackets.

1 How long have you been training to be an actor? (start)
When did you start training to be an actor?
2 How long ago did you meet your best friend? (since)
How long is it _____ your best friend?
3 I have been driving for six months. (began)
I _____ .
4 My sister keeps annoying me all the time. (always)
My sister _____ me.
5 How much experience do you have in playing tennis? (have)
How long _____ tennis?
6 I've never seen a better singer than him. (ever)
He's the best singer _____ .
7 The match only started a minute ago. (just)
The match _____ .
8 Clare has never acted on TV before. (first)
This is the _____ on TV.

3 Put the verbs in the correct tense.

Dogs 1) _have been_ (be) man's best friend from early times. We 2) _____ (always/read) about dogs that go missing and then take incredibly long journeys to find their owners. A few years ago, a stray dog in China 3) _____ (run) behind a group of cyclists for twenty-four hours. He 4) _____ (travel) over 1,500 kilometres! Happily, one of the cyclists finally 5) _____ (decide) to give him a home.

4 Use the clues to complete the crossword.

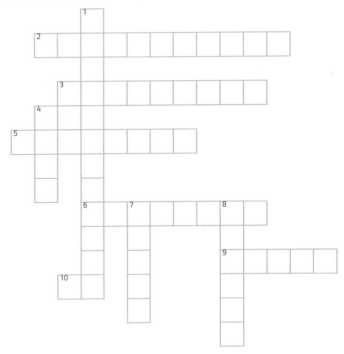

Across
2 A person who starts doing something that everybody else follows
3 An adjective for someone who seems relaxed and not worried about anything
5 _____ people enjoy meeting other people
6 This is another word for *brothers and sisters*.
9 An adjective for someone who is very careful what they choose and is difficult to please
10 If you give _____ something, you stop doing it.

Down
1 People sometimes have a love-hate _____ .
4 The past participle of *wear*
7 Another adjective for *courageous*
8 Another adjective for *talented*

LISTENING

1 Match the beginning of the sentences (1–6) with the endings (a–f).

1 I never liked that student ___c___
2 I was isolated at school _____
3 It's good to have new experiences _____
4 You should look beyond appearance _____
5 I want a friend to be totally honest _____
6 My sister and I argue sometimes _____

a and there's a lot of sibling rivalry!
b because it's hopeless if they don't say what they think.
c we just didn't hit it off.
d because they broaden your horizons.
e as it's easy to judge by first impressions.
f since I wasn't part of a friendship group.

2 ◀|| **1.1 Listen to an interview with Alan, who is talking about his ideas of friendship. Choose the correct answer, A, B or C.**

1 Alan says that meeting his best friend
  Ⓐ happened by chance.
  B was organised by a teacher.
  C helped him get on with his classmates.

2 What does Alan think about friendships on social media?
  A They're not as good as meeting face to face.
  B They tend to have more regular contact.
  C They break up more often.

3 According to Alan, what is the most important quality for a good friend?
  A being loyal
  B telling the truth
  C having a sense of humour

4 What does Alan think about people who are good listeners?
  A They provide valuable support, in his experience.
  B They may be interested for the wrong reasons.
  C They are great if they have similar ideas.

5 Alan talks about the incident with Jack to show that people
  A should always help each other.
  B should do their work at the right time.
  C should avoid judging by first impressions.

6 What does Alan say about how relationships with family compare with friends?
  A They never really change.
  B They can be more difficult to keep up.
  C They can be more argumentative.

SPEAKING SKILLS

1 Match the questions (1–7) with the topic areas (a–d). You will need to use some of the topic areas more than once.

TOPIC AREAS

a Future possibilities   c Friends
b Everyday life   d Free time

1 What time of the day do you like best? ___b___
  A In the morning I usually go to school, and in the evening I do my homework.
  B I usually feel energetic in the morning, so I prefer that to the afternoon when I feel sleepy.

2 How much time do you spend doing homework every evening? _____
  A I usually do about two hours, but sometimes it's more.
  B I have too much homework and I can't finish it all in an evening.

3 If you could live in another country when you're older, where would it be? _____
  A I'd love to live in Norway, because the scenery is so beautiful.
  B I visited Sweden once, and it is a beautiful place.

4 What would your ideal job be? _____
  A I'm very good at maths, so being a maths teacher would be perfect for me.
  B My sister is a doctor, but I don't really like hospitals much, so it wouldn't be good for me.

5 What kind of music do you enjoy listening to or playing when you're relaxing? _____
  A I don't like classical music very much, though I do play the piano.
  B I'm in to jazz, because it's very lively and also my brother plays the saxophone.

6 Tell us about a film you enjoyed watching in the cinema. _____
  A I loved Star Wars, which is science fiction, because it was so exciting.
  B I usually enjoy films that are full of action, like Star Wars, but I haven't seen it yet.

7 Who do you most enjoy spending time with? _____
  A I've got a small group of friends who I enjoy hanging out with. We all know each other well and we have a great time together.
  B I have a weekend job. I help my uncle in his shop on Saturday mornings.

2 Choose the correct answer, A or B, to the questions in Exercise 1.

WRITING

1 Read the task and choose the correct words to complete the statements (1–8).

> Your school is arranging exchange visits with another country. A student from that country, Sam, will come and stay with you for two weeks, and after that you will visit Sam. Read Sam's first email to you and write your reply.
>
>
>
>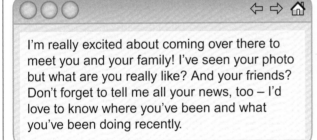
>
> ○○○   ⇦ ⇨ ⌂
>
> I'm really excited about coming over there to meet you and your family! I've seen your photo but what are you really like? And your friends? Don't forget to tell me all your news, too – I'd love to know where you've been and what you've been doing recently.

1 You need to write *an email/an essay*.

2 You are writing for *a teenager/an adult*.

3 Your style should be *formal/informal*.

4 You need to organise your writing into *paragraphs/headed* sections.

5 You need to give *two/three* pieces of information.

6 You are asked to describe *your family/your friends*.

7 To talk about recent activities you will probably mostly use the *present perfect/present simple* tense.

8 To describe yourself and your friends, you will probably mostly use the present *simple/past simple*.

2 Choose the informal sentence in each pair.

1 **A** Dear Sir,
  (**B**) Hi Sam.

2 **A** It was great to get your email yesterday.
  B Thank for your recent email, which I received yesterday.

3 **A** It will be very nice to meet you.
  B I can't wait to meet you!

4 **A** I am sure you will enjoy meeting my friends.
  B You're going to love my friends!

5 **A** You'll never guess where I went last weekend!
  B You will probably be surprised to hear where I went last weekend.

6 **A** I went to a party last night – it was really cool.
  B I went to a party last night which was very enjoyable.

7 **A** I look forward to hearing from you.
  B Hope to hear from you soon.

8 **A** Yours faithfully,
  B Best wishes,

3 Read the task again. Complete the paragraph with these words.

> big-headed ~~hang out~~ into outspoken
> rebel sense of humour trendy

> ○○○   ⇦ ⇨ ⌂
>
> You asked about my friends; there are three of them, and we always 1) *hang out* together. There's Oscar – he's 2) _____ dance and drama. He's really talented, but it's good because he never shows off or gets 3) _____ . He's very generous too, and so is Rebecca, my second friend. She's a bit of a 4) _____ though – very cool and 5) _____ (you should see her clothes!) and sometimes very 6) _____ – she just speaks her mind without thinking. Then there's James; he's laid-back and sociable and he's got a great 7) _____ . He's always making us laugh.

4 Write your answer to the task in Exercise 1. Write 140–190 words in an appropriate style.

Revision Unit 1

1 Complete the sentences with an appropriate preposition.

1 Where do you hang _____out_____ most weekends?

2 Are you addicted _____ rap music or do you hate it?

3 Do you get on well _____ most of your classmates?

4 What kind of bad behaviour puts you _____ people?

5 Would you find it easy to give _____ using your mobile phone?

6 Are you the kind of person who stands _____ from the crowd?

7 My brother is obsessed _____ skateboarding.

8 It's expensive trying to keep _____ with the latest trends.

2 Choose the correct answer, A, B or C.

1 I have a lot in _____ with my sister.
  A line   B common   C use

2 Well done, but don't let success go to your _____.
  A head   B heart   C brain

3 If you're independent, you like _____ your own thing.
  A being   B saying   C doing

4 I wish Paul didn't always _____ life so seriously!
  A make   B do   C take

5 I'm sorry if I _____ your feelings.
  A hurt   B damaged   C knocked

6 Keep your feet on the _____ and don't let success spoil you.
  A path   B ground   C earth

7 Shy people sometimes don't want to stand out from the _____.
  A group   B friends   C crowd

8 Clive wants everyone to notice him; he's a terrible _____.
  A show-off   B bully   C rebel

3 Choose the correct answer.

1 He was wearing *baggy, long pants/long, baggy pants* and a T-shirt.

2 I like *cotton, trendy T-shirts/trendy, cotton T-shirts*.

3 She's got some *blue, beautiful, denim jeans/beautiful, blue, denim jeans*.

4 My sister's bought herself *a fantastic, loose, woollen sweater/a woollen, fantastic, loose* sweater.

5 Dad's got several *cream, linen, plain suits/plain, cream, linen suits*.

6 The model was wearing a *stunning, red, knee-length dress/knee-length, red, stunning dress*.

7 George looked good in his *silk purple/purple silk* shirt and tie.

8 Clare liked that *short, tight, leather skirt/tight, leather, short skirt*, but her mum wouldn't let her buy it.

4 Use the correct form of the word in capitals to fill each gap.

1 Don't be so _____fussy_____! — FUSS

2 My parents love to _____ with friends in their free time. — SOCIAL

3 You don't need to be so _____ about everything! — SARCASM

4 My dad's jokes are actually quite _____. — FUN

5 Doctors need to be very kind and _____ people. — CARE

6 Fiona's a very _____ sort of girl, so she won't get into any trouble. — SENSE

7 My mum's so unselfish and _____! — THINK

8 Stop behaving like a _____ child! — SPOIL

5 Complete the collocations by matching the words.

1 sibling   a interests
2 love-hate   b trends
3 total   c mates
4 a household   d rivalry
5 sworn   e relationship
6 the latest   f opposites
7 common   g name
8 best   h enemies

6 Put the words in the correct order.

1 he / hours / is / It / left / since / three / .
   It is three hours since he left.

2 a / band / been / for / Has / in / long / she / the / time / ?

3 always / asking / bossy / girl / is / questions / that / Why / ?

4 Did / hear / I / just / said / what / you / ?

5 penfriend / Have / to / written / yet / you / your / ?

6 best / ever / film / have / I / is / seen / That / the / .

7 ages / did / discover / for / not / secret / the / We / .

8 a / am / getting / I / job / next / of / temporary / thinking / year / .

7 Complete the spaces in the text with an appropriate word.

8 Rewrite the sentences using the words in capitals.

1 He began painting some years ago.   FOR
   He has been painting ___*for a year*___ .

2 My friends have a habit of teasing me.   ARE
   My friends _____ me.

3 This is his first experience of   NEVER
   appearing on TV.
   He _____ on TV before.

4 It's ages since I've been to this park.   NOT
   I _____ this park for ages.

5 The band haven't played together   SINCE
   for a month.
   It's a month _____ together.

6 This watch is not mine.   BELONG
   This watch _____ me.

7 I haven't been to the cinema since July.   TIME
   The last _____ the cinema was July.

8 They've been here for ten minutes.   AGO
   They _____ .

9 I'm still reading.   NOT
   I _____ yet.

10 I need a reliable friend.   ON
   I need a friend I can _____ .

Girlfriend problems?

Calling all you guys out there! 1) ___*Have*___ you ever had problems choosing the right girlfriend? Are you good 2) _____ forming new relationships, or 3) _____ you sometimes get things quite wrong? Before you give 4) _____ on relationships completely, let me give you some advice. Many of you guys 5) _____ competitive and like showing off to your mates, right? Hanging 6) _____ with a beautiful girlfriend may seem like the ideal way to do this. Perhaps you think it makes you stand 7) _____ from the crowd? Well, it's not a clever idea at all! Just 8) _____ a girl looks good, it doesn't mean she has a personality. She may end up boring you to death! No, date a girl with a beautiful mind and then your friends will really envy you.

02 Wild

READING

1 Read the article and complete the sentences with these words.

> assistant   bear   ~~ecologist~~   endangered
> freelance   interfere   malaria   patient
> respect   uncomfortable

1 Paul is a biologist, or, more exactly, an
  ecologist .
2 He says you need to be very _____ to get good photos of animals.
3 He says if you don't _____ wild creatures, it could be very dangerous for you.
4 Sarah especially likes photographing animals that are _____ .
5 She points out that wildlife cameramen often have to wait in _____ positions.
6 She believes that people shouldn't _____ with nature, even if they see a sick animal.
7 Lee worked for a photographic company and then decided to go _____ .
8 He is scared of mosquitoes because they spread a disease called _____ .
9 Emma got started in her job when her employer's husband took her on as an _____ .
10 She was once almost attacked by a _____ .

2 Read the article again. For each question (1–10), choose the correct photographer (A–D). You can choose each person more than once.

Which person:

1 mentions wanting to help save animals from extinction?   _B_
2 is more afraid of a disease than being attacked by a large animal?   _____
3 mentions the importance of taking care when dealing with wild creatures?   _____
4 gives an example of a skill that a lone cameraman might need to survive in wild places?   _____
5 believes you must sometimes put yourself in a bit of danger to get a good photograph?   _____
6 was worried when he first decided to work for himself?   _____
7 is against stepping in to protect wild animals that are in trouble?   _____
8 is amazed how well animals can adjust to new surroundings over time?   _____
9 had an unexpected opportunity to work abroad while still a teenager?   _____
10 decided not to go to university after beginning a job in photography?   _____

PAUL   SARAH   LEE   EMMA

GOLD EXPERIENCE

WILDLIFE PHOTOGRAPHERS

A PAUL

As a wildlife photographer, I have one of the best jobs in the world. By photographing the wild world, I can share it with those who never get the chance to travel like I do. As an ecologist I'm always astonished by the ability of the Earth's creatures to adapt to different environments. It's this continual wonder that makes me love my job. You need eyes like an eagle or you miss the best shots ... and enormous patience because you often spend days waiting for the creature you want to film to appear. Getting a perfect shot is a chance in a million so it takes luck. You also need a healthy respect for your subjects; a minute's inattention could cost you your life.

B SARAH

As a wildlife photographer, I have to wake up much too early for my liking! I need to go out while it's still dark so I'm in the right position to start filming at daybreak. My favourite subjects for filming are endangered species – I want to make people realise how brilliant these creatures are and then help protect them. Comfort is certainly not part of this job! Getting the perfect shot might involve sitting in a freezing cold river, for example, or lying in thick mud. You need to know how to keep going alone in harsh environments – including repairing your vehicle if it breaks down in the middle of nowhere! Animals don't just pose for you, so you need to predict their behaviour, which is tricky, even if you're a qualified biologist. It's important to be detached; if you see an injured or sick animal your first instinct is to assist it. But the rule is that you must leave nature alone and not interfere. That's hard to do at times.

C LEE

When I told my parents I wanted to photograph nature as a career, they thought I was crazy. They wanted me to go university – and I was planning to – but before starting my course I got a holiday job with a photographic company, loved it, and gave up the idea of studying completely! The pay was awful, so after a year or two I was advised to go freelance. That was scary at first, because if you're self-employed there's no guarantee anyone will give you a job. But I was offered a job with a big TV company filming a famous wildlife series. People often ask me which I think is the most dangerous animal in the world. I tell them that for me it's not tigers, crocodiles or bears, but mosquitoes. Malaria can be a silent killer.

D EMMA

I didn't like school as a kid and spent all my time dreaming, and looking out of the window. I loved wild places and nature though. Anyway, I got a job working in the kitchens of a little restaurant and my boss introduced me to her husband George who was a wildlife cameraman. He told me all about his job and I couldn't wait to hear more. Then out of the blue George invited me to go to Africa with him, as his assistant! I was only 17. After that, I got offered a job filming big cats. Predators are my favourite animals – especially bears. They're very unpredictable. I remember once when I was still learning my trade, I camped out alone at night when a bear with huge claws came to my tent. I just managed to escape and the next morning I found the tent had been ripped to pieces! I'm not stupid, but in this job you have to take some risks to get good shots.

VOCABULARY
Wildlife

1 Complete the words in the sentences.

1 Diana doesn't fit in. She's such a teacher's p___e___t!
2 Animals like lions and wolves p_____y on other animals.
3 Most dogs are happy if you st_____ them.
4 Fishermen often sl_____er sharks in their thousands.
5 You can't stop yourself when you need to sneeze – it's a re_____x action.
6 Hedgehogs roll up in a ball when they're in danger – it's a def_____e mechanism.
7 I didn't use to like birdwatching, but now I'm h_____ed – I do it all the time!
8 A fish needs f_____s in order to swim properly.

2 Identify the animals in the pictures and complete the sentences below.

1 _F_ A ___gorilla___ is a great ape that can walk on two legs.
2 ____ A _____ can be extremely venomous.
3 ____ A _____ lives in the ocean and preys on other fish.
4 ____ A _____ has striped skin and striped fur.
5 ____ A _____ swallows stones and can regrow all its sharp teeth.
6 ____ A _____ hunts seals on the sea ice.
7 ____ A _____ has a hard shell and eats jellyfish.

3 Choose the correct answer, A, B, C or D.

1 To save endangered animals, we need to protect their _____ from destruction.
   A areas   B regions
   C homes   D habitats *(circled)*
2 The emission of _____ gases may be altering the climate of our planet.
   A greenhouse   B global
   C solar   D warming
3 Tigers are an endangered _____.
   A sort   B type
   C category   D species
4 Some dry places are becoming deserts because of _____ erosion.
   A land   B soil
   C ground   D earth
5 When there's a heat _____, there's a risk of forest fires.
   A stroke   B storm
   C wave   D rise
6 When we burn fossil _____, we pollute the atmosphere.
   A fires   B oils
   C caps   D fuels
7 Large parts of the rainforest are disappearing due to illegal _____.
   A cutting   B chopping
   C logging   D sticking
8 Our weather may get more extreme because of climate _____.
   A alteration   B change
   C movement   D wave

4 Choose the correct phrasal verb.

1 They've *set up/set by/set on* a new company in town selling solar panels.
2 If you *run up/run out of/run through* pet food, your dog won't be too happy!
3 My dad *gave out/gave off/gave up* driving last year – he goes everywhere by bike now.
4 That tree is dying; they'll need to *cut it up/cut it down/cut it off* soon.
5 Companies should make products that can be repaired, not just *thrown down/thrown away/thrown up*.
6 The music is too loud in here! Can you *turn it up/turn it in/turn it down*, please?

GRAMMAR
Post tenses

1 Choose the correct verb form.

1 I *was walking/walked/had been walking* for ten minutes when I came across the injured fox.

2 We sheltered in our tent because *it rained/it was raining/it had rained*.

3 My neighbour used to have a pet snake, but it *was always escaping/had always been escaping/had always escaped*, so he got rid of it.

4 The bull *saw/was seeing* the dog, *chased/was chasing* it across the field and *was then throwing/then threw/had then thrown* it up in the air.

5 The cheetah was exhausted because it *was running/had been running/ran* at top speed for quite some time.

6 The park was in complete darkness because the sun *had gone/went/was going* down.

7 I bet you *were feeling scared/felt scared/had felt scared* when the lion appeared in front of you!

8 *Did the tiger kill/Had the tiger killed/Had the tiger been killing* the cub by the time the ranger arrived?

2 Complete the sentences with the correct form of the verb in brackets.

1 When we got back from the safari, a TV company *was waiting* to interview us. (wait)

2 Because it _____ all day, we were able to see the bear's tracks very clearly. (snow)

3 While I _____ on a rock, I spotted a shark circling out at sea. (sit)

4 Zoologists trekked through the mountains for days because they _____ to find a snow leopard. (want)

5 The whale was the most amazing animal we _____ ! (ever see)

6 After a week in the jungle, the cameramen _____ millions of photos. (already/take)

7 The minute we _____ that the elephant was in trouble, we ran to get help. (realise)

8 It was ages since I _____ a horse. (last/ride)

9 How long _____ the deer before the lions arrived? (you/watch)

10 We were excited because we _____ on a wildlife holiday before. (never/go)

3 Use the prompts to make correct sentences.

1 How long / you / dive / before / you / see / the turtle?
   How long had you been diving before you saw the turtle?

2 As we watched, the zebra / lift / its head and / look / at us.

3 They could see that the cat / already eat / the mouse / because / there / be only bones left.

4 While / the biologists / explore / the cave, / they / discover / a rare species of bat.

5 She / scream / very loudly / when / she / see / the scorpion?

6 Volunteers / rescue / the injured seal and / keep / it in a sanctuary until it / be / healthy again.

7 By the time she / get / her camera out, / the leopard / disappear.

8 The wolves / follow / the buffalo / for an hour / before the snowstorm / arrive.

4 Complete the article with one word in each space.

DANGER IN THE DARK!

Animals 1) *have* escaped from captivity many times over the years. However, a few years 2) _____ there was a mass escape of wild animals. The state police described it as the worst event they 3) _____ ever encountered. They had all 4) _____ hoping for a quiet night when the first calls came into the office. Callers reported seeing bears, big cats, and other dangerous beasts which 5) _____ running loose along the highway! At first the police 6) _____ not know whether to believe the stories, but when they visited the wild animals preserve they saw the fence 7) _____ broken and the cages were empty. It took a long time to round up the animals – big cats were hiding up trees in the dark so the situation was extremely dangerous! People had to to stay indoors and schools were closed 8) _____ several days. A free holiday then, but what a scary reason to get off class!

USE OF ENGLISH
Vocabulary: offixes

1 Write the opposite meaning of these adjectives in the correct box below.

> ~~logical~~   experienced   formal
> happy   honest   legal   obedient
> polite   possible   practical   relevant
> responsible   reversible   satisfied x2

Il-	Ir-	Im-
illogical		

In-	Dis-	Un-

2 Complete the sentences with the correct form of the word in capitals.

1 I'm _unhappy_ about the numbers of animals that are endangered.   HAPPY
2 People who drop rubbish in the street are so ....! RESPONSIBLE
3 Driving above the speed limit is not just ...., it is bad for the environment, too.   LEGAL
4 Those plans won't work because they are too ....   PRACTICAL
5 If global temperatures rise by more than 2%, the effects on the planet might be ....   REVERSIBLE
6 The zookeeper who was attacked by the tiger was young and ....   EXPERIENCED
7 My puppy is really ...., so I'm taking him for proper training classes.   OBEDIENT
8 Companies that lie about the amount of energy they use are being ....   HONEST

3 Use the clues to complete the crossword.

Across
1 A violent crash involving two or more cars
5 A word that means *not bothered*
8 If you don't have an alarm clock, you may do this.
9 Jeans and T-shirts are an .... way to dress.

Down
2 An .... is someone who owns or runs a factory or company.
3 Another word for *rude*
4 If something is ...., you pay too much for it.
6 You need a lot of imagination and .... to be a great artist.
7 Something like a box or bowl that you keep things in

4 Complete the text with the correct form of the words in capitals.

Designing for nature

For decades 1) _scientists_ have warned us that global 2) .... is a major threat to our planet. There is a danger that our planet will overheat and that the resulting natural disasters may 3) .... life on earth. The materials designers and technologists use to manufacture products must be chosen carefully. Most metals are easy to 4) ...., so these are fine to use. The plastic used in some kinds of plastic 5) .... can be reused as well, but oil-based plastic is not biodegradable, so anything made with this material can be a major cause of 6) ....

SCIENCE
WARM

DANGER

CYCLE

CONTAIN

POLLUTE

USE OF ENGLISH
Grammar: used to, get used to, would

1 Complete the sentences by matching the parts.

1 As a small child, I always

2 Did you

3 Will you ever

4 Tanya can't get

5 Years ago, I would

6 Adam used

7 We'll never

8 Are you

a used to living in the country.

b getting used to working in a zoo?

c use to keep chickens?

d get used to eating insects!

e to work as a wildlife cameraman.

f get used to sleeping on the ground?

g never go near a spider.

h used to help my mum feed the chickens.

2 Choose the correct answer, A, B or C.

1 We're not used _____ horses.
   A to ride   B riding   **C to riding**

2 Did you know that my grandad _____ a vet?
   A would be   B used to be   C use to be

3 When we lived on a farm, we _____ help Dad milk the cows.
   A would always
   B always would
   C use always to

4 As a child, _____ scared of dogs?
   A would you be
   B did you use to be
   C use you to be

5 Our pet rabbit _____ spoiled by all of us.
   A always used to be
   B was always used to be
   C always would be

6 The boys _____ working with animals.
   A aren't used to
   B don't use to
   C used not to

7 When my sister was a baby, she _____ elephants laid eggs!
   A would think
   B used to thinking
   C used to think

3 Complete the text with one word in each space.

When we were younger, our parents used to take us into the countryside 1) _____*at*_____ the weekend.
We 2) _____ walk a few kilometres and then sit down to picnic. Once, we stopped to eat in a large field.
We 3) _____ only just unpacked our picnic when we heard a deafening roar. We looked round quickly – and saw a huge bull watching us! This bull was clearly not 4) _____ to humans. It had 5) _____ sleeping peacefully and 6) _____ not appreciate being woken up. From the way it moved its head, we could see it 7) _____ planning to charge.
8) _____ the time we'd jumped to our feet, the bull was nearly upon us. What on earth were we going to do?

4 Complete the verbs in each sentence.

1 I was scared so my heart was b _e_ _a_ t _i_ _n_ g very fast.

2 We were wearing wet suits because we'd been d _____ g.

3 My brother picked up the snake although I b _____ g _____ him not to.

4 Sandra's hamster had got out of its cage and d _____ r _____ d.

5 The hunters sl _____ t _____ r _____ d hundreds of sharks.

6 While we were sitting in the forest, a deer suddenly c _____ s _____ through the trees near us.

7 Our teacher o _____ i _____ for us to go on a wildlife trip.

8 We listened carefully until we _____ a _____ d the sound of horses' hooves.

LISTENING

1 🔊 **2.1 Listen to five journalists talking about animal rescues. Choose the animal that performed each rescue. You do not need three of the animals.**

> a bear   a dog   dolphins   a gorilla   ~~lions~~
> a pig   a shark   a wolf

1 Mali was rescued by ___*lions*___
2 The man was rescued by ___
3 Tom was rescued by ___
4 Stella and Karl were rescued by ___
5 Bella was rescued by ___

2 🔊 **2.2 Listen again. For each journalist (1–5), choose the thing they mention (a–h). You do not need three of the letters.**

Speaker 1 ___*f*___
Speaker 2 ___
Speaker 3 ___
Speaker 4 ___
Speaker 5 ___

a ignoring official warnings
b being trapped by fallen objects
c not having enough time to follow advice
d acting sensibly to prevent injury
e acting strangely to attract attention
f helping to protect a victim from capture
g taking unnecessary risks
h anticipating a danger that became real

SPEAKING SKILLS

1 Complete the conversation with these words.

> about   are   agree   does   don't   how
> ~~let's~~   mean   opinion   personally   right
> that's   think   won't

A OK, 1) ___*let's*___ think about this idea – cycling instead of driving. I don't 2) ___ that's a very good idea. But 3) ___ about you?

B Well, 4) ___ I think it could do some good. In my 5) ___ , the atmosphere is so polluted that anything we can do to cut down on dirt and gases in the air has got to be good, 6) ___ you think?

A Yes, 7) ___ a good point, but surely traffic doesn't contribute that much to air pollution these days, 8) ___ it?

B Maybe you're 9) ___ . Perhaps it's more about using up energy. Think about it – if you're riding everywhere, you're not using up oil or gas or electricity, 10) ___ you?

A I see what you 11) ___ but personally I don't think you and me riding around everywhere is going to make a big difference to the world's environmental problems!

B I have to say that I 12) ___ with you there. But it will help us get fitter, 13) ___ it?

A True! Right – what do you think 14) ___ this next idea?

2 Put the words in the correct order.

1 start / Let's / shall / this / one, / we / with /
   ___*Let's start with this one, shall we*___ ?
2 afraid / I'm / don't / I / agree / you / with /
   ___ .
3 isn't / problem, / it / the / That's /
   ___ ?
4 point, / but / there's / to consider / That's / a / good / something else /
   ___ .
5 what / mean / you / see / I /
   ___ .
6 I / you / I agree / have to / say / that / with /
   ___ .
7 but / OK, / does it / that doesn't / the problem, / really solve /
   ___ ?
8 Maybe you're / sure / not / I'm / right, / but /
   ___ .

WRITING

1 Read the task from an exam and choose the correct answer, A, B or C.

You have seen this announcement in an international magazine for schools.

Readers' stories

Would you like to feature in next month's magazine? Win our story competition and we'll publish your story and your photo. Your story must end with this sentence:
What an amazing person! Alice sighed to herself when she got home that evening.

Your story must include:
• a camera
• a difficult situation

Write your story.

1 Who is going to read the story?
  A young children
  B teenagers
  C adults

2 Why are you writing the story?
  A to entertain and inform
  B to educate
  C to persuade

3 Will your readers expect your story to be
  A lively?
  B impersonal?
  C confusing?

4 Will your story contain mainly
  A present perfect tenses?
  B past tenses?
  C present tenses?

5 How many paragraphs is an effective story likely to have?
  A one
  B two
  C three or more

2 Read the question and choose the correct answers.

Which *four* of the following would you do in a real FCE exam?

a read the question carefully and underline important points
b make a paragraph plan and make sure you include both the bulleted points
c make up the plot as you go along
d decide on the plot before you start
e replace the bulleted points with your own ideas if it makes a better story
f think of a dramatic way to start your story
g spend half the available time deciding on your plot

3 Write your answer to the exam task in 140–190 words, using an appropriate style. Use an idea from the photos or your own ideas.

Revision Unit 2

1 Complete the table with the missing word forms.

	Verb	Adjective	Noun
1	emit	xxxxxx	emission
2	conserve	conservative	
3	xxxxxx		environment
4	erode	eroded	
5		threatening	threat
6		dangerous/	danger
7	pollute		
8		industrial	(person)

2 Complete the sentences with the correct form of the word in capitals.

1 Cutting down forests can cause soil _erosion_ . **ERODE**

2 Dad has _____ to sell my dog if it doesn't stop barking all night! **THREAT**

3 Fumes from cars and lorries cause a great deal of _____ . **POLLUTE**

4 _____ organisations work to highlight the dangers posed by greenhouse gases. **ENVIRONMENT**

5 As more countries _____ , the need to protect our planet grows more urgent. **INDUSTRY**

6 Many zoos regard _____ as one of their major roles. **CONSERVE**

7 Polar bears are increasingly seen as an _____ species because the ice they hunt on is melting. **DANGER**

8 Industries guilty of the _____ of greenhouse gases may be fined a lot of money. **EMIT**

9 Illegal _____ is destroying large sections of this planet's rainforests. **LOG**

10 Some industries still use too much packaging, such as unnecessary plastic food _____ . **CONTAIN**

3 Complete the collocations by adding one word.

1 If we want to be 'green', instead of driving cars we should use _public_ transport.

2 A long period of extremely hot weather is called a heat _____ .

3 _____ fuels like coal and oil are formed from the remains of prehistoric plants and animals.

4 Our seas are getting warmer due to climate _____ .

5 Some weather forecasters say global _____ will give Europe wet, cold summers for many years.

6 _____ power is the result of converting sunlight into electricity.

7 Sea levels are rising because the Arctic _____ caps are melting.

8 _____ gases like carbon dioxide increase the temperature of our planet.

4 Complete the sentences with an appropriate preposition.

1 Madison set _up_ her own film company.

2 They've cut _____ our beautiful palm trees to make way for a car park.

3 It's quite warm today so you can turn _____ the heating a bit.

4 One day we may run _____ of fossil fuels.

5 Don't forget to switch _____ the lights if you're the last to leave.

6 Why not give your old clothes to charity shops instead of throwing them _____ ?

7 I'm going to give _____ eating meat and become a vegetarian.

8 We must go _____ fighting to conserve nature and never give up.

9 I have asked Finn to turn his music _____ twice, but it's still too loud.

10 I don't like Gina because she puts me _____ all the time in front of my friends.

5 Choose the correct answer, A, B or C.

1 They were the scariest animals we _____ .
A ever saw
B were ever seeing
C had ever seen ⟨selected⟩

2 The zoo _____ have so many animals as it has now.
A didn't use to
B wouldn't
C used to not

3 By the time I got home, the sun _____ down.
A had already been going
B had already gone
C already was going

4 The company was fined because they _____ chemicals in the river for months.
A had dumped
B were dumping
C had been dumping

5 We nearly killed the frogs because we _____ caring for amphibians.
A weren't used to
B didn't use to
C used not to

6 While you _____ this morning, I was out birdwatching.
A had still slept
B were still sleeping
C had still been sleeping

6 Complete the article with one word in each space.

Bob the street cat

James Bowen used 1) _to_ be a lonely busker. Every day he 2) _____ sit in the street and play his battered old guitar to earn money. He was 3) _____ to being alone. But that all changed 4) _____ Bob the cat arrived at his flat. James didn't really want a pet, but as Bob had been sitting on his doorstep 5) _____ three days, he invited him in. Bob was badly injured – a fox or another cat 6) _____ attacked him – so James nursed him back to health. After that, Bob followed him everywhere, even on the bus! Soon they 7) _____ even busking together and Bob became a star on YouTube!

7 Complete the second sentence so it has a similar meaning to the first, using the word in capitals. Do not use more than five words.

1 On my arrival, I started exploring my surroundings.
AS
I started exploring my surroundings _as soon as I arrived_ .

2 It was his first experience of seeing tigers.   BEFORE
He _____ .

3 Their journey took three days so they were very tired.
FOR
They were very tired because they _____ _____ three days.

4 During the filming, the cameramen got stung by bees.
WHILE
The cameramen got stung by bees _____ _____ .

5 They haven't seen the gorilla for two days.   LAST
It's two days _____ a gorilla.

6 The weather changed before my departure.   LEFT
By _____ ,
the weather had changed.

7 The bull charged before the walkers had finished eating their picnic.
STILL
The bull charged while the walkers _____ _____ picnic.

8 It was the best experience of her life.   EVER
It was the best experience she _____ _____ .

8 Find ten words on the topic of the environment. The words go across, down or diagonally. The first letter of each word is highlighted.

b	i	m	e	l	g	h	a	n	d	k	n	j	f	c
w	w	i	l	d	l	i	f	e	u	o	x	m	k	e
c	c	l	i	m	a	t	e	a	i	z	z	j	o	r
s	p	j	y	w	n	m	p	t	v	g	n	w	g	o
n	o	k	h	e	n	d	a	n	g	e	r	e	d	s
q	l	u	n	z	a	v	m	n	l	b	y	l	b	i
y	l	h	l	l	r	s	w	k	v	q	d	o	k	o
n	u	f	d	e	o	p	h	p	e	i	y	g	s	n
s	t	o	s	u	f	e	a	i	c	l	o	g	c	l
p	i	n	k	l	r	c	b	g	o	s	q	i	o	k
l	o	p	c	i	d	i	i	f	l	h	b	n	r	g
c	n	e	p	p	e	e	t	u	o	y	t	g	l	u
i	w	m	b	q	s	s	a	v	g	k	q	r	p	q
g	u	h	l	q	h	n	t	a	y	b	j	p	i	q

READING

1 **Read the story and match (1-6) with (a-f) to complete the sentences.**

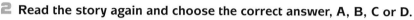

1 Bob was very keen on
2 Bob was still clearly nervous on
3 Emily didn't feel nervous on
4 The other passengers were quiet while
5 The crew gave instructions just before
6 Bob and Emily were the first to notice

a the noisy take-off.
b the crew made final preparations.
c the idea of space travel.
d the mysterious object in space.
e the days leading up to the trip.
f the day of the trip.

2 **Read the story again and choose the correct answer, A, B, C or D.**

1 From the first paragraph, we understand that Emily
   A was firm in her resolution to go on the space trip.
   B was angry at Bob for suggesting the space trip.
   C regretted agreeing to join Bob on the space trip.
   D was not sure about going on the space trip.

2 The word *spooked* (line 22) suggests that
Bob had been
   A training hard.
   B unable to sleep.
   C feeling unwell.
   D feeling scared.

3 When she first stepped onto the space ship, Emily
   A enjoyed being a celebrity.
   B was feeling worried about Bob.
   C showed signs of anxiety.
   D couldn't breathe in her spacesuit.

4 As Emily waited for the final countdown, she
   A refused to think of anything.
   B wondered if she would enjoy space.
   C was unable to stop panicking.
   D kept her mind on the present.

5 When the booster rockets were fired, the passengers
   A made a deafening noise.
   B were scared into silence.
   C found the effects disturbing.
   D thought there was something wrong.

6 When the travellers first experienced weightlessness, Emily
   A asked Bob to remind her about something.
   B worried about what might happen next.
   C made a critical comment to Bob.
   D felt reassured about the trip.

Stranded in space

'Whatever possessed us to volunteer for this?' Bob muttered to Emily as he struggled to walk in his bulky grey spacesuit. 'What if something goes horribly wrong?'

'Oh, how many more times?' Emily muttered
5 under her breath. After all, it was Bob who had seen the advertisement on the Space Trek website and jumped at the chance to take this 'journey of a lifetime'. She had been slower to warm to the idea, torn between the desire for adventure
10 and her apprehension at the obvious risks. Bob's enthusiasm had won out though and once the decision was made, for her there was no looking back.

'Shh!' she told him, in the most reassuring
15 voice she could manage. 'You're going to scare the others. We're in expert hands. What can possibly go wrong?'

'We'll all feel better once the flight starts,' one of their fellow travellers whispered
20 encouragingly. But was that actually the case? Bob, normally the most courageous of men, had been completely spooked in the last few days. He'd been strangely silent during the day, while regular nightmares
25 left him trembling and bathed in sweat.

Worrying about Bob had prevented Emily from dwelling too much on her own reservations regarding the trip. But now, as she struggled aboard the spaceship, panting
30 under the weight of her padded suit, helmet and breathing equipment, Emily could feel her heart pounding. Turning, she managed a smile and a somewhat shaky wave at the press photographers thronging below, took one
35 last look at the familiar things of Earth and then stepped inside the flight capsule. The pilots, two experienced space veterans, were already seated in front of their instrument panels carrying out pre-flight checks. Multi-coloured lights flashed
40 on and off as a voice from a distant control room gave final instructions.

Emily and Bob took their seats alongside their fellow 'passengers'. Apart from the crew, there were six of them and they sat three in a line on
45 each side of the spaceship. In front of them were large round windows from which, in just a while, they would view the wonders of space. As the countdown to take-off approached, there was silence in the capsule. 'What was it like to be
50 stranded in space?' Emily wondered. Shuddering, she dismissed the thought from her brain. Such last-minute doubts were a waste of time, she knew. Better to focus on the here and now.

'Three minutes to go. Visors down. Hold on to
55 your seats, folks!' a voice informed them through their headphones. Seconds later there was a mighty roar and a sudden rush of air hit the spaceship – the adventure had begun!

Looking through the window, Emily watched
60 the sky turn from blue to purple until, finally, the spaceship entered the blackness of space.

'Preparing to fire the booster rockets. We're going into orbit everyone!' A deafening roar confirmed the next stage of their flight
65 was underway. Emily grabbed Robert's hand as the vehicle hurtled through space. The woman opposite jerked upright in her seat in terror while others exchanged nervous looks. The noise was overwhelming, but just as Emily thought she
70 couldn't stand it any longer, it began to decrease until finally there was nothing but silence. The travellers gazed at each other, almost in disbelief. They'd made it so far, safe and sound! Their worried frowns relaxed into smiles, and they
75 applauded wildly.

On a word from the crew, they unstrapped themselves from their seats and experienced the weightlessness of space, floating around the cabin. 'What did I tell you?' Emily teased Bob as she
80 somersaulted through the air.

But Bob wasn't listening to her. His eyes were fixed on the window beside them, or rather on something outside the window that was approaching at breakneck speed.
90 A meteorite? But surely a lump of rock would not be so perfectly shaped or so stunningly lit as this? And what was that noise? It sounded like ... no, it couldn't be ... through her headphones, Emily heard someone – or something – speaking
95 in a language she'd never heard before. What was going on?

VOCABULARY
Science and technology

1 Complete the sentences with these words.

> aliens   doomed   gravity   ~~planet~~
> predictions   robot   satellite   weird

1 The Earth is not a star; it is a _____planet_____ .
2 The very first _____, called Sputnik, was launched into space back in 1957.
3 From time to time, people claim they have seen _____ arrive on Earth in flying saucers!
4 Without the force of _____ we would all float off into space.
5 I find the idea of parallel universes really _____ .
6 Don't you wish they'd build a _____ that would do your homework for you?
7 If you ever fell into a black hole, you could never escape – you'd be _____ !
8 Physicists can't prove all their theories, but they have made some amazing _____ about the nature of the universe.

2 Match a word from the box with each of the lists below.

> astronomy   chemistry   geology
> mathematics   ~~physics~~   technology

1 _____physics_____
  black holes
  parallel universe
2 _____
  numbers
  patterns
  shapes
  problems
  logical
3 _____
  machines
  gadgets
  equipment
  kits
4 _____
  solar eclipse
  planets
  stars
  space
  galaxy
5 _____
  test tubes
  experiments
  acids
  gases
  substances
6 _____
  rock formations
  fossils
  dinosaur bone

3 Choose the correct word, A, B, C or D.

1 My chemistry teacher says I'm _____ a lot of progress.
   A doing   B having
   C getting   **(D)** making
2 The technician hasn't managed to _____ the air conditioning yet.
   A heal   B cure
   C fix   D solve
3 I wish I'd _____ more attention in class!
   A done   B paid
   C made   D lent
4 Have you written up the experiment we _____ in class yesterday?
   A did   B got
   C made   D used
5 Turn down the heating to _____ energy.
   A preserve   B save
   C spare   D limit
6 Can somebody tell me how to _____ this machine?
   A control   B run
   C perform   D work
7 Our new chemistry teacher got the job because she _____ lots of previous experience.
   A got   B owned
   C did   D had
8 Some chemicals have _____ missing from the laboratory!
   A gone   B ended
   C resulted   D come

4 Choose the correct preposition.

1 The teacher told us to get *up/in/on* with our work.
2 My experiment turned *up/in/out* better than I thought it would.
3 They're going to shut *off/down/out* our local chemical factory.
4 The chemist's attempts to heat the substance ended *up/out/of* as a disaster.
5 Can you take *round/on/over* this task from me while I answer the phone?
6 We're not allowed to copy; we've got to come *up/in/over* with our own ideas!

GRAMMAR
The future

1 Choose the correct answer, A, B or C.

1 While you're having your interview tomorrow, I _____ my grandparents.

   A am visiting   **(B)** will be visiting   **C** visit

2 As soon as I _____ my new telescope, I'll take a course in astronomy.

   A will get   **B** am getting   **C** get

3 At some point in the future, scientists _____ send a manned spacecraft to Mars.

   A are going to   **B** go to   **C** will be going to

4 We're going to test the liquid after it _____ .

   A is cooling   **B** will cool   **C** cools

5 What _____ this evening? Would you like to come out with me?

   A will you do   **B** are you doing   **C** do you do?

6 While my dad _____ the lecture, I'll be sitting in the audience!

   A is giving   **B** will be giving   **C** will have given

2 Complete the mini dialogues with the appropriate form of the verb in brackets.

1 **A:** Don't worry. I'll switch out the lights when I _____ *go* (go).

   B: Thanks!

2 **A:** _____ (you/not go) to the Science Fair this afternoon? You'll be sorry if you miss it!

   B: Don't worry, I put my name down ages ago!

3 **A:** What time are they expecting you at the planetarium?

   B: The performance _____ (start) at 9 a.m. sharp – I've checked on the programme. We'll get there some time before that.

4 **A:** We _____ (sit) in a biology lesson this time tomorrow – as usual! What about you?

   B: Oh, we've got a holiday day tomorrow. Hurray!

5 **A:** By the time it comes back to earth next week, that satellite _____ (travel) round the Earth for six months.

   B: Wow, that's incredible!

6 **A:** I _____ (study) science at university. That's my plan, anyway.

   B: Well good luck. I hope you do well at it!

3 Use the prompts to make correct future sentences.

1 I / go / cinema tonight
   I am going to the cinema tonight.

2 By this time next year / we / move house.

3 At 10 a.m. tomorrow you'll be at home, but I / fly / over the Pacific!

4 I / send / you a text as soon as I / hear / the news.

5 The teacher says he / buy / some new test tubes / when / he / get / the chance.

6 Hurry up! The chemistry lesson / start / in five minutes!

7 After we / finish / learning about frogs, / we / go on / to another bit of the biology syllabus.

8 My sister Tanya / leave / school / by the time / I / be / in my final year.

4 Complete the sentences with the correct word.

1 It's possible that the teacher won't give us homework, but it isn't _____ *likely* _____!

2 We're _____ to get in to the gig because we don't have tickets.

3 Do you know what time the plane is due _____ land?

4 We _____ going to take the bus, but Sally has decided to walk instead.

5 It's very _____ to snow, so don't go walking in the mountains.

6 Hurry up! The lecture _____ about to start.

7 I _____ going to call my parents for a lift, but I couldn't find my mobile.

8 My mum's _____ to leave for work, so if you need to speak to her you'll have to hurry.

USE OF ENGLISH
Vocabulary: dependent prepositions

1 **Complete the sentences by matching the parts.**

1 A test tube is a finger-shaped and U-shaped glass object

2 A thermometer is a glass device

3 Scales are instruments

4 A beaker is a cylindrical container with a flat bottom

5 A telescope is an instrument

6 A calculator is a device

a used to measure the weight of things.

b used to perform sums and calculations.

c used to help you view faraway objects, like stars.

d used to hold small quantities of chemicals.

e used to measure temperature.

f used to stir, mix, and heat liquids in.

2 **Complete the sentences with a correct preposition.**

1 Recently, there's been an increase ___in___ the temperature on our planet.

2 Our teacher insists _____ accuracy.

3 Who is responsible _____ breaking the test tube?

4 My sister has a real talent _____ physics.

5 I think I'd benefit _____ a long holiday!

6 Can I rely _____ Paul or not?

7 We were ashamed _____ our chemistry test results.

8 There was no lack _____ interest when our teacher suggested a trip to the Science Museum.

3 **Complete the article with the correct form of the words in capitals.**

4 **Find ten words on the topic of science. The words go across, down or diagonally. The first letter of each word has been highlighted for you.**

u	t	s	b	k	r	t	e	l	e	s	c	o	p	e
u	s	k	g	d	f	s	a	t	e	l	l	i	t	e
n	d	e	n	n	w	y	l	w	q	h	h	f	e	o
i	i	x	l	p	t	i	a	i	f	x	b	r	n	d
v	v	p	f	w	h	f	b	r	e	l	q	t	t	b
e	f	e	z	d	e	r	o	u	i	f	n	e	c	g
r	g	r	x	r	e	x	r	e	q	e	n	d	h	l
s	s	i	e	k	o	p	a	t	m	a	k	e	n	e
e	e	m	a	b	i	b	t	n	l	p	k	e	q	y
m	t	e	v	c	g	i	o	p	n	z	i	j	t	v
c	b	n	d	a	h	r	r	t	t	l	r	f	j	e
s	l	t	e	l	i	i	y	k	a	z	n	p	l	l
t	f	g	f	v	f	h	u	v	r	q	i	u	s	s
l	d	u	n	k	s	z	a	r	t	i	s	t	l	x
u	g	e	k	t	g	r	a	v	i	t	y	z	u	h

Life on Mars?

Year by year, our little planet is becoming 1) _overcrowded._ As the human population continues to grow, 2) _____ are looking for planets which humans could colonise. One popular 3) _____ is that Mars will be our new home. However, it is icy cold and has very little carbon dioxide. At present, humans would be 4) _____ to survive there. But the big difference in the atmospheric 5) _____ of Earth and Mars hasn't stopped people from dreaming! One 6) _____ experts have made for heating up the planet is to build 'greenhouse gas factories'. They say these factories could take in carbon dioxide and give out oxygen, just as plants do on Earth. As 7) _____ as it may seem, these ideas may become reality one day. However, humans are 8) _____ to be living on Mars for many centuries to come.

CROWDED

SCIENCE

PREDICT

ABLE

CHEMIST

SUGGEST

CREDIBLE

LIKELY

USE OF ENGLISH
Grammar: future in the past

1 Choose the correct answer, A or B.

1 I'm not about to handle that snake!
   (A) I'm not going to do it.
   B I don't know how to do it.

2 You're likely to fail if you don't try harder.
   A It's probable you'll fail.
   B There's a small chance you'll fail.

3 I'm not due to see the headmaster until 4 p.m.
   A I have no intention of seeing him.
   B He's not expecting me until then.

4 I wasn't going to apologise to Sarah, but there we are!
   A I apologised.
   B I didn't apologise.

5 The train was due to leave at 11 a.m.
   A According to my opinion
   B According to the timetable

6 It's unlikely to rain.
   A It probably won't rain.
   B People don't want it to rain.

7 The movie is about to start.
   A It's going to start at any minute.
   B It's already started.

8 They were going to train as astronauts.
   A They did their training.
   B They didn't do their training.

2 Choose the correct answer, A, B or C.

1 The project might be ready on time, but it's _____ .
   A unsure   B impossible   (C) unlikely

2 The rain started as the tennis match was _____ to begin.
   A likely   B around   C about

3 They _____ going to launch the rocket today, but it's been cancelled.
   A were   B are   C weren't

4 I'm just _____ to get on the train, so I'll have to text you when I've found a seat.
   A about   B due   C likely

5 I thought you were _____ to meet me last night as planned. What happened?
   A due   B going   C about

6 I'm very sorry, but my essay is _____ to be finished on time.
   A impossible B unsure   C unlikely

3 Complete the text with one appropriate word in each space. Use any word *once* only.

www.newfirst.com

Scientists have recently come up with 1) ___*an*___ amazing invention. Imagine the scene. You 2) _____ about to rob a bank – but then a policeman comes and stands right next to you. You're unlikely 3) _____ try and rob the bank now, correct? But the invention I'm 4) _____ to describe might make robbery a lot easier in the future! I actually saw this wonderful bit of technology at a special video demonstration. The demonstration was 5) _____ to take place at 09.00 prompt, so I got to the university 6) _____ good time. At the start of the demonstration, a cat climbed into a tank. That's not very exciting, we thought. What we didn't realise was that the cat 7) _____ about to vanish in front of our eyes, by means of an 'invisibility cloak'! This new device hides objects by bending light in different directions. Sadly for robbers, however, it 8) _____ unlikely to be in the shops any time soon!

4 Correct the word in italics in each of these sentences.

1 The exam results are due *for* be published today!
   The exam results are due to be published today!

2 You're *likely* to see a lot of stars if it's cloudy tonight.
   _____

3 Mum's *about* to go on a lecture tour next month.
   _____

4 We *are* going to take our holiday in June, but we've had to change the date to July.
   _____

5 Paul wasn't *due* to ask Sonya out, but he couldn't stop himself.
   _____

6 Sh! The lecture is just *ready* to start.
   _____

7 According to the timetable, our plane is *likely* to take off in ten minutes' time.
   _____

8 Look out! That car was just *due* to run you over!
   _____

LISTENING

1 Which two things are <u>not</u> usually found in museums?

> cafés   exhibits   films   fitness machines
> guides   information   reading rooms
> travel brochures   shops   workshops

2 🔊 **3.1** Read the task in Exercise 3 and think which topics, (a–h) you may hear about. Listen and tick (✓) the topics in Abbi's presentation.

a   Things to see in the museum ✓
b   Things to do in the museum ____
c   The atmosphere in the museum ____
d   The cost of going to the museum ____
e   Space exploration ____
f   Wildlife ____
g   Going to the museum shop ____
h   Environmental problems ____

3 🔊 **3.2** Abbi is making a presentation to some schoolchildren about a visit to a science museum. Listen again and complete the sentences with a word or short phrase.

1   Abbi had not expected it to be very _noisy_ inside the science museum.
2   Abbi uses the word ____ to describe how she found the atmosphere in the museum.
3   Abbi was sorry that the discussion about ____ was not part of their study programme.
4   The landscape on Mars looked ____ , in Abbi's opinion.
5   Abbi says she didn't mind feeling ____ when she was in the flight simulator.
6   Abbi regretted not having time to see the section on ____ when she was exploring on her own.
7   The only one who enjoyed seeing the ____ . was Abbi.
8   All the students enjoyed the ____ they made in the café.
9   Abbi was surprised to find a ____ in the museum.
10 Abbi was glad she bought a ____ as a souvenir of the visit to the museum.

SPEAKING SKILLS

1 Complete the conversation with these words.

> ~~agree~~   instance   look   sure   true   with

A Some people say that science and maths are the most important subjects at school. Do you 1) _agree_ ?

B I'm not 2) ____ that I do really. I mean, it's 3) ____ that we need good engineers and scientists, but there are other priorities too. For 4) ____ , if you 5) ____ at the increasing importance of international communication, then languages are vital too.

A I'm 6) ____ you on that. I love science but education needs to be broader than that.

2 Put the words in the correct order.

1   sure / this / I'm / one/ about / not /
    I'm not sure about this one .
2   think / It's / what / know / to / hard / to /
    ____ .
3   that / must / Surely / about / agree / you /
    ____ ?
4   one / minds / this / on / I'm / two / in / this /
    ____ .
5   couldn't / more / I / Yes, / agree /
    ____ .
6   to / two / question / There / this / sides / are /
    ____ .
7   I've / of / before / that / thought / never /
    ____ .
8   tricky / answer / really / That's / to / a / question /
    ____ .

3 Match the phrases (1–6) with the functions (a–f).

1   I agree up to a point. _d_
2   I'm completely with you on that. ____
3   I've never thought about that before. ____
4   If you consider X, for instance ____
5   I believe that ____
6   How do you feel about it? ____

a   giving an example
b   giving an opinion
c   asking for an opinion
d   partially agreeing
e   totally agreeing
f   giving a reaction to the question

WRITING

1 **Read the homework essay question. Put the sentences (a–d) from a student's introductory paragraph in the correct order (1–4).**

> HOMEWORK
>
> Governments should stop spending money exploring space because there is no point to it. Do you agree?
>
> Notes
> Write about:
> • advances in science
> • cost
> • your own idea

a So should we give up exploring the universe and concentrate on them? ....

b Somehow I don't think so. ....

c Meanwhile a lot of people back here on Earth have little or no money to live on. ....

d Governments are spending huge sums of money on sending satellites, rockets and even humans into space. ...1...

2 **Choose the correct sentence, A or B.**

1 **A** Firstly, a lot of new inventions have resulted from the work done by space scientists.
   B In the beginning, a lot of new inventions have resulted from the work done by space scientists.

2 **A** It's rubbish when people say that space travel is too expensive to justify.
   B I don't agree with the idea that space travel is too expensive to justify.

3 **A** In spite of, this is not the only reason I think space travel is a good thing.
   B However, this is not the only reason I think space travel is a good thing.

4 **A** For me, it's just a waste of time and money.
   B In my opinion, it's just a waste of time and money.

5 **A** At the end, I would argue that as humans we need to explore our world.
   B Finally, I would argue that as humans we need to explore our world.

6 **A** On balance, I have to say that I think space travel benefits mankind.
   B With thought, I have to say that I think space travel benefits mankind.

7 **A** On the one hand, space travel is expensive, but on the other hand, it could be the answer to some of the Earth's problems.
   B On the one hand, space travel is expensive, but as well as this it could be the answer to some of the Earth's problems.

8 **A** Space travel is expensive. What's more, it can be very dangerous.
   B Space travel is expensive. Plus, it can be very dangerous.

3 **Write your answer to the essay in 140–190 words, using an appropriate style.**

Revision Unit 3

1 Complete the sentences.

1 A person who studies numbers and shapes and does calculations is a(n) _mathematician_ .

2 A person who controls the making of something in a factory is a(n) _____.

3 A person who studies rocks, soils, and minerals and how they have changed over time is a(n) _____.

4 A person who is the first to think of an idea for a new product and then designs or makes it is a(n) _____.

5 A person who makes, or repairs, modern machines and equipment, like computers, is a(n) _____.

6 A person who studies the structure of things like acids and liquids and mixes them in a laboratory is a(n) _____.

7 A person who studies natural forces, such as light, heat, and movement – and black holes in space is a(n) _____.

8 A person who studies the movement of the stars and planets is a(n) _____.

2 Identify the objects in the pictures.

A	B

C	D

E	F

3 Choose the correct answer, A, B, C or D.

1 Now take the _____ and weigh the rock you have chosen.
   A beaker   B test tube
   C scales *(circled)*   D thermometer

2 The laboratory _____ we do in our normal science classes are sometimes quite dangerous.
   A experiences   B trials
   C examinations   D experiments

3 Our lab assistant had to _____ over the experiment because our teacher was feeling ill.
   A get   B take
   C carry   D come

4 Our _____ is just one of the many groups of stars that make up the universe.
   A planet   B star
   C galaxy   D world

5 Clare's very _____ of how she behaved in our science class yesterday.
   A embarrassed   B sorry
   C apologetic   D ashamed

6 Jessica _____ on washing all the test tubes by herself.
   A stressed   B insisted
   C determined   D wanted

7 Ben's school can't build a new lab because it's suffering from a _____ of cash.
   A lack   B gap
   C space   D loss

8 My dad thinks I'd _____ from extra biology lessons.
   A benefit   B succeed
   C advance   D progress

4 Complete the words in the sentences.

1 Some people believe they've seen flying saucers, but I find the whole idea completely i _n_ _c_ _r_ ed _i_ _b_ _l_ _e_ .

2 If you're really interested in how rocks are formed, you should think about becoming a g _____ l _____ i _____ .

3 It's very _____ l _____ y that people will be living on Mars any time soon.

4 Can you pour the liquid into that _____ a _____ r?

5 Sadly, some of the p _____ d _____ scientists make may never come true.

6 Without the force of _____ v _____ , objects wouldn't fall to the ground.

5 Rewrite the sentences, using the word in capitals. Do not use more than five words.

1 The satellite will travel thousands of kilometres before it goes into orbit.
   TRAVELLED
   By the time the satellite goes into orbit, *it will have travelled* thousands of kilometres.

2 The demonstration will start very soon.
   ABOUT
   The demonstration ....

3 The movie will finish before you get there.
   HAVE
   By the time you get there, ...

4 The invention probably won't go on sale.
   UNLIKELY
   The invention .... go on sale.

5 What is the departure time for the plane tomorrow?
   DOES
   What .... tomorrow?

6 According to this leaflet, the museum should open in ten minutes' time.
   DUE
   According to this leaflet, the museum .... in ten minutes' time.

6 Complete the text with one word in each space.

Danger from Space!

Over the years there have been many predictions 1) *about* our planet, Earth. According to some Hollywood movies, a near-Earth object, like an asteroid or a comet, 2) .... likely to collide with the Earth one day soon. Relax! No asteroids are 3) .... to hit the Earth – well, not 4) .... the next few decades anyway. However, over coming years NASA scientists will 5) .... working on a plan to deal with any such dangers. They hope that by the end of their project, they will 6) .... worked out how to change the orbit of any asteroid that threatens our planet. During the project, they 7) .... be thinking about how to put an early warning system in place. Then, if the asteroid is small enough, they may be able to send 8) .... robotic spacecraft into space to alter its course.

7 Use the clues to complete the crossword.

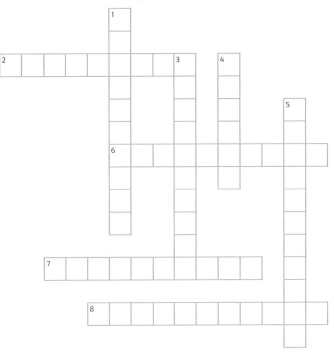

Across

2 A machine that circles the Earth and helps us predict the weather
6 A scientist who studies the stars and the planets
7 A statement about what may happen in the future
8 You use this to measure the temperature

Down

1 You use this to work out the answer to your multiplication problem
3 The name given to a scientific test done in a laboratory
4 The name given to creatures from another world
5 A word that means *filled with too many people or things*

04 Dream jobs

READING

1 Match the words (1–5) with their definitions (a–e).

1 a careers adviser ___c___
2 a volunteer _____
3 an accountant _____
4 a live chat _____
5 a CV _____

a a typed conversation on the Internet
b a person who works without a salary
c someone who helps people choose the work they do
d a short written summary of your qualifications and work experience
e a person whose job is to deal with financial records

2 Read the four texts and write true (T) or false (F).

1 Don is good at writing and literature ___F___
2 Don has always wanted to go to university _____
3 Alice loves working with computers _____
4 Alice wants to be a lawyer _____
5 John is good at sport _____
6 John has always known what he wanted to do _____
7 Ellie likes working with people _____
8 Ellie is happy getting more qualifications _____

3 Complete the sentences with these words from the texts. You do not need one of the words.

> a loss   dead-end   got into   in the meantime   ladder
> lived up to   looked back   lookout   stay on
> ~~stick to~~   work   worlds   worth

1 I hate my temporary job, but I won't leave – I'll ___stick to___ it till the end of the year.
2 I don't know what to do with my life – I'm at _____ at the moment.
3 It's always good to get your foot on the _____ by starting work.
4 It was a real _____ job – it led nowhere, so I left.
5 It's _____ getting some work experience before you start your career.
6 You can get some _____ experience while you're a student.
7 I'm planning to _____ at school next year to get more qualifications.
8 I'll have to wait for a good opportunity but _____ I'm going to carry on studying hard.
9 I love what I'm doing now – I've never _____ or regretted choices I've made.
10 The job I'm doing now hasn't _____ my expectations – it's boring.
11 I've got the best of both _____ because I can earn money and study too.
12 When you're job hunting, you have to be on the _____ for any opportunities.

4 Read the texts again. For each question (1–10), choose the correct person (A–D).

Which young person:

1 regrets a decision they made about school? ___D___
2 was reassured about financial matters? _____
3 contacted a careers adviser because they were feeling frustrated? _____
4 mentions a lack of careers advice at school? _____
5 has changed their career plans completely? _____
6 was pleased that volunteering would help their career? _____
7 found talking to people already doing the job useful? _____
8 says they feel more confident knowing their adviser is always there to help? _____
9 was unwilling to go to another country to do voluntary work? _____
10 appreciated the way the adviser dealt with them? _____

A Don (aged 19)

I'd always thought I wanted to do something with computers, because I was obsessed with them when I was young. I'd been studying games design at college for several months, but it wasn't living up to my expectations. I was at a loss, not knowing where to turn. I'd had some help from teachers at school but I guess they thought with my background I should stick to computing. I went on the web and searched for careers advice. I found a site offering live chat with an adviser, who suggested something I hadn't thought of – being an accountant. I've always been good with numbers, and he said I could get an apprenticeship with a firm so I wouldn't have to go to university. That was something I'd been worried about, because I wanted to make money, not spend it as a student! I found an apprenticeship quickly and I love it – I've never looked back to my computing days. There'll be loads of exams and studying, but I'm on the bottom rung of the ladder.

B Alice (aged 18)

I've already got a place at university to study law, but that doesn't start until the autumn. I was working part-time as a waitress to fill the time but honestly it seemed a real dead end and not rewarding in any way. I wanted to do something better so I contacted a careers adviser, who suggested I did some volunteer work – not because that would make me money but because it would look good on my CV and would give me some more valuable work experience. Some people I know volunteered abroad, but that didn't appeal to me. I found an opening helping local people to use computers – older people and those with no technical know-how – and it's great. It's only two afternoons a week, so I can still be a waitress in the evenings. So I've got the best of both worlds: earning money and getting experience of helping people from different walks of life, which is well worth having if you want to be a lawyer.

C John (aged 15)

I'm unusual in that I've always known what I want to do – my ambition is to be a police officer. I looked for information on line, and found a live chat service with a careers adviser. Because I'm still young, there isn't much careers advice provided for my year at school. The adviser told me what qualifications I'd need, and the physical tests I'd have to get through. Apparently there isn't just one way of getting in to the service – I could stay in education and go to university or look for part-time or temporary work to give me life experience. He suggested working as a volunteer in the local community, which I thought sounded a great idea. I've already found information about that, but I think I'll have to wait until I'm 16 to start. One thing that really helped me was talking to local police officers; I got some idea of what's really involved. I feel positive about my future, and I'm working hard at school to get good grades and improve my physical fitness.

D Ellie (aged 17)

I chose to stay on at school to get extra academic qualifications, which I now reckon was the wrong thing to do. I'll stick it out, but I've been on the lookout for any part-time job that could be helpful in the future. I've already got a Saturday job in a small clothes shop, but what I ultimately want to do is be a retail manager. I'm pretty good with people and I know I have the right sort of personality, so I went to a careers adviser for suggestions. He told me to make sure my CV was up-to-date, and that the more experience I could get in retail the better. He didn't tell me what to do, just presented me with different options and left it up to me. I found that very helpful, especially as he didn't patronise me. Although I haven't got anything definite fixed up right now, I'm sure about what my aims are, and it's good to know I can contact the adviser again whenever I need to. Once I've finished school I'll apply to companies directly, but in the meantime I'm going to keep on with my job in the shop – it gives me experience and money.

VOCABULARY
Work

1 Choose the correct answer, A, B or C.

1 My uncle works in a department _____ .
   A shop   (B) store   C showroom

2 Our local factory is trying to _____ new staff.
   A recruit   B rent   C gain

3 Don't worry! The company will train you in the _____ you need for the job.
   A qualifications   B duties   C skills

4 Our teacher is applying for the _____ of headmaster in another school.
   A contract   B post   C work

5 Bob isn't a qualified workman yet; he's an _____ , so he gets training while he works.
   A assistant   B applicant   C apprentice

6 They only _____ Jack last month and now they've dismissed him!
   A hired   B rented   C featured

7 Make sure you read the _____ carefully before you agree to sign it.
   A post   B contract   C application

8 Dad's job involves going round to clients and _____ the company's new projects to them.
   A recruiting   B featuring   C promoting

2 Complete the sentences with these verbs in the appropriate form.

> be made   conduct   earn   fit   ~~manufacture~~   write

1 I've got a summer job with a company that _manufactures_ cars.

2 I hope my headmaster has _____ me a really good reference.

3 We _____ a survey in class yesterday to find out which jobs are the most popular.

4 My brother won't tell me how much he _____ per month in his job.

5 I thought I'd found my friend a job, but she says she doesn't _____ the job description.

6 My aunt has just _____ redundant.

3 Complete the words in the sentences.

1 If you've always known what career you want, then you have a v _o_ _c_ _a_ _t_ _i_ _o_ _n_ .

2 An official agreement between two or more people. c _____ t

3 Doctors are people who make a c _____ out of medicine.

4 If you want a job, you need to fill in this _____ p _____ t _____ form.

5 The people who form most of the staff of a company are the e _____ e _____ .

6 They've taken my brother on as an a _____ t _____ in a local carpentry business.

7 It's easier to find a good job if your head-teacher writes you an excellent r _____ r _____ .

8 They're reducing the number of staff, so a lot of workers are going to be made r _____ d _____ t.

4 Choose the correct word.

1 My brother's relying *in/by/on* Dad to get him to work on time.

2 Thousands of companies are closing down, so many people are *from/out of/under* work.

3 The cashier charged the customer the wrong amount *in/from/by* mistake.

4 Students are *under/in/on* a lot of pressure to acquire good job skills these days.

5 We're not allowed to ring Mum *at/in/on* work because it disturbs her too much.

6 You'll be *on/for/in* trouble with the boss if you come to work late.

7 Make sure you arrive *on/in/at* time for the planning meeting!

8 Dad says he's been *on/under/in* his feet all day and he needs to sit down.

9 I enjoy working in marketing because I can come *on/up/down* with new ideas.

10 I don't like it when my manager goes away because I end *up/of/out* doing a lot of her work!

GRAMMAR
Gerunds and infinitives

1 Choose the correct form of the verb.

1 I've decided *studying/study/to study* law when I leave school.
2 It's not worth *apply/applying/to apply* for that job because it doesn't pay well.
3 *Nurse/To nurse/Nursing* is a great vocation.
4 My sister's job involves *promote/promoting/to promote* beauty products.
5 My mum doesn't want me *leave/to leave/leaving* home for good.
6 I intend to spend a year *travel/travelling/to travel* before I go to university.
7 Do you happen *to know/knowing/know* what the salary is?
8 Dad's boss made him *to work/work/working* overtime last week.

2 Complete the sentences with the verbs in brackets in the correct form.

1 Have you considered _taking_ (take) a temporary job?
2 I didn't intend _____ (annoy) you.
3 I'm looking forward to _____ (hear) from the company.
4 His dad made him _____ (cut) his hair before the interview.
5 Did you manage _____ (change) the time of the interview?
6 I hope I don't end up _____ (be) late for my first day.
7 My friend wanted me _____ (help) her with her application.
8 James would rather _____ (stay) at home than work.
9 I'd suggest _____ (not/wear) those torn jeans for your interview!
10 Her boss let her _____ (go) home early today.

3 Complete the sentences with a preposition and put the verb in brackets in the correct form.

> about   for   ~~from~~   in x2   on   up   with

1 He would benefit _from preparing_ (prepare) more carefully before interviews.
2 Maria ended _____ (work) in a beach café.
3 My dad was responsible _____ (recruit) more staff for his company.
4 Paul insists _____ (stay) late if he has work to finish.
5 How _____ (help) me with this paperwork?
6 We had difficulty _____ (get) the photocopier to work.
7 Nurses have to put up _____ (do) shift work even if they hate it.
8 I'd like to be involved _____ (save) animals from extinction.

4 Complete the text with one word in each space.

A Job with a Difference

Are you looking 1) _forward_ to leaving school? Would you like 2) _____ do one of the most unusual jobs in the world? Well, how 3) _____ becoming an ostrich babysitter? You won't be 4) _____ too much pressure – you just 5) _____ to sit in a field full of ostriches and make sure they don't fight! Or perhaps you'd prefer to 6) _____ a furniture tester? For this job, all you need to do while you're 7) _____ work is to test chairs and beds – by sitting or lying on them! It's the perfect job for a couch potato – you know, someone who likes sitting and watching TV all the time – and so much nicer than being 8) _____ your feet all day!

USE OF ENGLISH
Vocabulary: suffixes

1 Use the clues to complete the crossword.

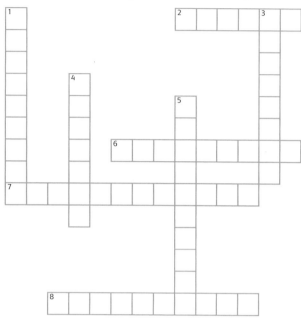

Across
2 If a policeman arrests you, you may need help from this person.

6 A person who is willing to work for no money

7 A person who checks people in and out of a hotel

8 If your business needs help dealing with finance, ask this person.

Down
1 A person who tells us about the news on the TV

3 A person or company that pays people to do a job

4 You may go to this person for special advice

5 A person who writes for a newspaper

2 Complete the table.

	Noun	Verb	Adjective
1	demand	demand	*demanding*
2	xxxxx	flex	
3	idiot	xxxxx	
4	practice	practise	
5	competition	compete	
6	knowledge	know	
7	motivation	motivate	
8	sense	xxxxx	/sensitive

3 Complete the sentences by changing the words in capitals into adjectives.

1 We were hoping to repair the machine, but the damage is not __*reversible*__. **REVERSE**

2 It's _____ to spend time with a careers adviser before you choose your career. **SENSE**

3 What you did was completely _____. **IDIOT**

4 Terry must be telling lies; his excuse is completely _____. **BELIEVE**

5 Saving lives as a doctor must be really _____. **SATISFY**

6 A job in a factory can be quite _____. **REPEAT**

7 If your job involves being on your feet all day, it must be so _____. **TIRE**

8 Technologists have to be quite _____ these days. **INVENT**

4 Complete the article with the correct form of the word in capitals.

Are you looking for an 1) __*interesting*__ job? Or maybe you've found one already? As you probably know, the job market today is very 2) _____. So if you're lucky enough to be invited for an interview, it's 3) _____ to consider how you can make the best impression. First, make sure you arrive on time. If you're 4) _____ on public transport, make allowances for delays and cancellations. Secondly, be careful how you look. Even if the employer is looking for someone 5) _____, it's best to avoid looking too way-out, like having a Mohawk haircut! Next, memorise what you have written on your resume. You'll look rather 6) _____ if you can't remember what you said there. Your employer will want you to be 7) _____ so it's important to answer questions fully. Don't make long speeches though. And finally, don't worry! Interviews may sound scary, but if you prepare well they can turn into really 8) _____ experiences.

INTEREST

COMPETE
SENSE

DEPEND

CREATE

IDIOT

COOPERATE

ENJOY

USE OF ENGLISH
Grammar: verb patterns

1 Complete each pair of sentences with the correct form of the verb in capitals.

1 TAKE
A: Oh no! I forgot _____to take_____ our dinner out of the freezer!
B: I'll never forget _____taking_____ my boss's phone home by mistake. How embarrassing!

2 SPEAK
A: The manager stopped _____ when Dad's mobile phone rang.
B: The manager stopped _____ to a technician about the problem.

3 GET
A: We tried _____ an interview with the TV presenter, but without success.
B: If your computer won't let you access the Internet, try _____ a new router.

4 PHONE
A: Did you remember _____ the company manager?
B: I can't remember _____ the repair shop, but I'm sure I did.

5 GET
A: I like _____ together with friends. We always have fun together.
B: Our teacher likes us _____ to class early.

2 Make correct sentences from the prompts.

1 I / try / tell my boss about the problem but I / not able / find him.
I tried to tell my boss about the problem but I
wasn't able to find him.

2 Only yesterday, the manager / warn / staff / not touch / the broken switch.
_____

3 He / stop / work at the factory when he / get / a better job.
_____

4 My last teacher / always / encourage me / work hard.
_____

5 Please / not expect me / work / evenings.
_____

6 I / not remember / the boss / tell me that / but I suppose he did.
_____

3 Identify the five sentences which contain a mistake and correct them.

1 Did you remember posting my letter as I requested? ✗
Did you remember to post my letter as I requested?

2 We stopped getting more petrol as we had nearly run out of fuel.

3 If your computer develops a problem, try switching it off and then on again.

4 Can you remember to suck your thumb when you were younger?

5 Please don't encourage George misbehaving.

6 I really wish I could stop to bite my nails. It's an awful habit!

7 I'm trying to ring Sarah but I can't get a signal.

8 You must remind me paying you the money I owe you.

4 Rewrite the sentences using the words in capitals. Use between two and five words, including the word given.

1 Trips to the cinema are enjoyable.
LIKE
I _like going to_ the cinema.

2 I must continue to save for my holidays.
STOP
I must not _____ for my holidays.

3 Barbara is certain that she put the keys on the table.
REMEMBERS
Barbara _____ on the table.

4 Mum texted to say I shouldn't be late for my interview.
REMINDED
Mum _____ late for my interview.

5 Tom's boss said he must continue without taking a break.
STOP
Tom's boss said he couldn't _____ .

6 Her train was late so she couldn't get to work on time.
TRIED
She _____ work on time, but she couldn't because her train was late.

LISTENING

1 📢 **4.1 Listen to part of a radio programme with Tom, a careers adviser. Choose the *three* pieces of advice that he gives about job interviews.**

1 Go to bed early the night before.
2 Memorise your CV or resumé. *(circled)*
3 Wait to be invited to sit down.
4 Avoid very short skirts if you're a girl.
5 Switch off your mobile phone.
6 Don't chew gum or sweets.

2 📢 **4.2 Listen again and choose the correct answer, A, B or C.**

1 What does Tom say about job interviews?
  A Doing research before an interview is useful. *(circled)*
  B It's unlikely you'll enjoy going for an interview.
  C You shouldn't over prepare for an interview.

2 Tom thinks that preparing your answers before your interview …
  A would be considered weird.
  B wouldn't help you very much.
  C would put you at an advantage.

3 When attending an interview, Tom advises against …
  A dressing extremely formally.
  B wearing neat, informal clothes.
  C wearing unconventional T-shirts.

4 Tom feels job applicants should not …
  A make contact with the other applicants.
  B relax by checking text messages.
  C get to the interview before time.

5 To control last minute nerves, Tom says it's a good idea to …
  A focus on something peaceful.
  B breathe more quickly.
  C draw a picture calmly.

6 Tom says that one thing you should avoid during the interview is …
  A lying about your qualifications.
  B being too detailed in your answers.
  C asking the interviewer too many questions.

7 Tom feels that the worst thing to do in an interview room is to …
  A stare at the interviewer too much.
  B move about nervously.
  C fail to pay attention.

SPEAKING SKILLS

1 **Look at the photos and choose the correct answer, A or B, to complete the sentences.**

1 The photos .... two young people at work.
  A show *(circled)*   B are showing
2 To me, ... look like students.
  A both   B the two
3 The boy has to wear special clothes .... the girl can wear what she likes.
  A although   B whereas
4 I .... the girl's job is more boring than the boy's job.
  A could think   B imagine
5 They .... quite happy and relaxed in their jobs.
  A look   B look like
6 Their jobs must be tiring – I .... , they're on their feet all day so that must be hard.
  A intend   B mean

2 Match the sentences (1–6) with the definitions (a–f).

1 I think for this task we're supposed to discuss what the people have to do in their jobs. _____
2 Both the photos show students at work. _____
3 The girl looks relaxed, whereas the boy is probably under more pressure. _____
4 I imagine the boy is probably serving dinner. _____
5 The girl is serving a customer. _____
6 I think being a waiter takes patience. I mean, you have to deal with difficult customers. _____

a speculating about what is happening
b saying what is different between two things
c discussing how to do the task
d saying what is similar between two things
e giving an opinion and then clarifying/explaining your idea
f describing exactly what is happening

3 Prepare to talk about these photos. What do you think they enjoy/don't enjoy about their jobs?

4 Time yourself talking about the photos. Can you talk for one minute?

WRITING

1 Choose the correct word or phrase to link the sentences.

> Although   As a result   As well as this   ~~whereas~~
> Because of   However   In spite of   Otherwise

1 TV actors often become famous, ____whereas____ scriptwriters rarely become well-known.
2 _____ her salary isn't fantastic, Anna adores her job.
3 It was lucky Carlos saw the advertisement. _____ he might never have found out about the job.
4 Alex always loved performing. _____ this, he decided to audition for a part in a movie.
5 John's business moved to North America. _____, he found himself living in Chicago.
6 My uncle invented a number of things. _____, he never managed to interest anybody in manufacturing them.
7 Helen started designing clothes. _____, she opened her own boutique in our local high street.
8 Nobody thought Jack would succeed as a racing driver. _____ this, he spent all his free time practising on the local race rack.

2 Read the advertisement. Choose the *four* things from the list (1-8) that your article should have.

> We want to know about the person whose job you would most like to have.
>
> Send your article to us and we'll post the best one on our website.
>
> Write 140–190 words.

1 very formal language
2 a variety of linkers
3 sections with clear headings
4 a catchy title
5 mainly past tenses
6 a range of grammatical structures
7 a maximum of two paragraphs
8 details or explanations

3 Look at the advertisement again and write your answer.

Revision Unit 4

1 Choose the correct answer, A, B or C.

1 The boys stripped _____ their clothes and jumped in the river.
   A out   **B** off   **C** down

2 If the store closes down, all the staff will be _____ redundant.
   A found   **B** made   **C** kept

3 I enjoy having a _____ every morning during the holidays.
   A sleep-in   **B** stay-in   **C** lie-in

4 My dad always encourages me to _____ high in life.
   A aim   **B** shoot   **C** fire

5 Emma is extremely _____ so she would make great speeches as a politician.
   A attractive   **B** winning   **C** articulate

6 The producer left no _____ unturned in his search for a leading lady.
   A stone   **B** rock   **C** pebble

7 Standing under a tree when there is lightning about is crazy and could _____ you in hospital.
   A finish   **B** land   **C** end

8 Working every day of the week is not my _____ of heaven!
   A version   **B** idea   **C** dream

2 Find ten words on the topic of work. The words go across, down or diagonally. The first letter of each word is highlighted.

r	m	b	o	c	o	n	t	r	a	c	t	c	r	c
r	e	f	e	r	e	n	c	e	y	v	m	o	s	l
p	j	k	r	e	c	r	u	i	t	d	z	n	d	j
o	w	z	o	c	y	t	x	s	i	j	o	s	t	f
b	e	f	z	e	k	w	p	t	s	i	c	e	e	k
r	i	s	e	p	e	g	e	j	t	a	a	r	p	n
v	o	t	j	t	n	h	b	a	g	d	l	v	v	t
n	d	a	h	i	p	f	c	u	s	l	e	a	c	v
i	q	f	l	o	l	i	v	u	l	e	x	t	r	g
u	x	f	d	n	f	a	q	m	y	a	g	i	s	y
m	i	w	l	i	o	e	w	o	c	x	i	o	u	x
s	i	l	l	s	p	t	l	y	b	a	p	n	l	b
x	m	a	z	t	t	p	z	v	e	z	n	i	m	p
c	u	h	c	u	m	q	o	j	o	r	o	q	c	s
q	o	i	k	e	d	r	e	d	u	n	d	a	n	t

3 Complete the sentences with the correct form of the word in capitals.

1 All the *employees* who work in the mines have to wear hard hats because the job is so dangerous.   EMPLOY

2 Did the headteacher write you a good job _____?   REFER

3 You need to list your _____ on the form they sent you.   QUALIFY

4 The _____ with the best skill set got the only job.   APPLY

5 It's hard to find a job these days, so it helps if you're _____.   COMPETE

6 Fiona's not very _____; in fact, she spends all her time dreaming!   PRACTICE

7 Let me know if you see a _____ job for me when you're on the Internet.   SUIT

8 My teacher's really _____ about the careers I can choose.   KNOWLEDGE

4 Match words from each list to make logical collocations.

1 get
2 be made
3 conduct
4 earn
5 fill in
6 learn
7 manufacture
8 play
9 recruit
10 sign

a a contract
b a new skill
c a product
d a role
e a salary
f an application form
g a survey
h redundant
i staff
j a new job

5 Complete the sentences by putting the verbs in brackets into the correct form.

1 My interests include drama and *reading*. (read)

2 I'm interested in _____ (know) what qualifications you need to be a vet.

3 Her mum stopped her from _____ (get) a summer job.

4 Dan promised _____ (help) me fill in my application form.

5 My dad's job involves _____ (meet) lots of people.

6 We happened _____ (see) the company director in the street yesterday.

6 Rewrite the sentences using the words in capitals. Use between two and five words, including the word given.

1 There's no alternative to working long hours.   PUT
We have to _put up with working_ long hours.

2 My employer wouldn't give me permission to leave work early.   LET
My employer .... work early.

3 John is not accustomed to doing shift work.   USED
John .... shift work.

4 The staff were keen on me making a speech at the meeting.   WANTED
The staff .... a speech at the meeting.

5 It might be a good idea to get some work experience before you decide on your future career.   SUGGEST
I .... work experience before you decide on your future career.

6 Applying for a job without the necessary skills is a waste of time.   WORTH
It .... a job if you don't have the necessary skills.

7 The careers adviser didn't keep me waiting for too long, thank goodness.   MAKE
Thank goodness the careers adviser didn't .... too long.

8 Do you fancy going to a movie after work?   ABOUT
How .... after work?

7 Complete the text with the best answer, A, B, C or D.

	A		B		C		D	
1	any	(B)	no	C	some	D	few
2	wish	B	ambition	C	vocation	D	intention
3	allow	B	permit	C	enable	D	let
4	in	B	at	C	on	D	from
5	before	B	for	C	under	D	over
6	on	B	with	C	onto	D	by
7	succeeds	B	endures	C	intends	D	manages
8	ends	B	comes	C	brings	D	takes

A Rewarding Career

I have 1) _no_ idea what to do when I leave school. I envy people who know exactly what career they want to follow from an early age. If you have a definite 2) .... – for the religious life, for example, or for nursing – that must be great. My mum always wanted to be a nurse because it was a job that would 3) .... her help others. She works in a busy emergency department so she sees people who are 4) .... all sorts of trouble. This means she is 5) .... a lot of pressure all day. She's 6) .... her feet all day, too – she must walk several kilometres every week! I don't know how she 7) .... to keep going, but she does - and she never complains, either! Nurses can retire at the age of sixty in my country, but I bet Mum 8) .... up working until she's seventy.

8 Complete the conversation with the correct form of these verbs.

> be   do   find   ~~go~~   not/worry
> phone   walk   work

Sam: How was your work experience interview, Ann?

Ann: Getting there was the worst bit. We'd planned 1) _to go_ by bus, but there was a strike.

Sam: Oh no! Did you end up 2) .... all the way?

Ann: No, thank goodness. We managed 3) .... a taxi. It cost a fortune, though!

Sam: Oh! Well, you couldn't help 4) .... late in that case.

Ann: No, and luckily the boss was lovely and told me 5) ....

Sam: And how did things go after that?

Ann: It was great. They asked me all the usual questions, like what job I want 6) .... when I leave school and whether I've ever had experience of 7) .... in a shop before. They seemed really interested and they've promised 8) .... me later to say when I can start!

Sam: Brilliant! Well done, Ann!

READING

1 Read the article and choose the correct answer, A, B or C.

1 Nicola watched boxing every week on TV with her father.
    A True   **B** False   **(C)** Not given

2 Nicola's father taught her to box.
    A True   **B** False   **C** Not given

3 There were only boys in her first class.
    A True   **B** False   **C** Not given

4 Nicola needs to use her brain when she boxes.
    A True   **B** False   **C** Not given

5 Nicola's serious injury happened during a fight.
    A True   **B** False   **C** Not given

6 The law used to be against women boxing.
    A True   **B** False   **C** Not given

7 At the 2012 Olympics, women's boxing had few supporters.
    A True   **B** False   **C** Not given

8 Huge numbers of girls watched the women's boxing at the Games.
    A True   **B** False   **C** Not given

9 Nicola isn't considered a good role model.
    A True   **B** False   **C** Not given

10 A lot of girls have asked Nicola for advice about boxing.
    A True   **B** False   **C** Not given

2 Read the article again. Choose which sentence (a–g) fits each space (1–6) in the text. You do not need one of the sentences.

a Say that to Nicola, and she'd tell you that you're missing the point.

b Her ultimate success in the Olympics was still a faraway dream though.

c Her trainers treated her as an equal, which was fine by her.

d Nicola knows there are still people who oppose female boxing.

e When the bell goes she knows she's on her own, fighting for herself.

f Luckily for Nicola there was an afterschool boxing class, and she was invited to join in.

g How did she manage to come back from that?

3 Choose the correct answer, A, B, or C. The answers are all words from the article in the Students' Book, page 55.

1 Boxers try to hit each other with their _____ .
    A ankles
    (B) fists
    C wrists

2 My dad's a farmer and my eldest brother is hoping to follow in his _____ .
    A feet
    B shoes
    C way

3 Last night I _____ downstairs, careful not to wake my parents, and stepped outside into the moonlit street.
    A sneaked
    B rushed
    C bumped

4 When mum saw what my little brother had been _____ while she was away, she punished him severely.
    A down to
    B away with
    C up to

5 If you're _____ , you will want to beat other people at sport in a fair way.
    A big-headed
    B competitive
    C aggressive

6 One of my friends _____ on Saturday to pick up the tablet she'd lent me.
    A dropped by
    B went round
    C fell in

7 You won't be very healthy if you insist on eating _____ food.
    A rotten
    B waste
    C junk

8 Some people believe girls should be _____ from boxing because it's too dangerous.
    A banned
    B finished
    C controlled

TREAT HER WITH RESPECT!

★ ★ ★ ★ ★ ★ ★ ★ ★ ★ ★ ★ ★ ★ ★ ★ ★ ★ ★ ★

When Nicola Adams won an Olympic gold medal for boxing, it was a dream come true. She had grown up with two brothers and was used to being the only girl. Gentle by nature, she still shared her boxing-mad father's love of boxing. When he watched legendary boxers like Muhammed Ali fight on TV, she was just as glued to the screen as he was. She loved the excitement of it all, and wanted to do the same.

Her chance to try out the sport came when she was just twelve. Her mum had an aerobics class and couldn't find a babysitter, so she took Nicola along to the gym with her. 1) __f__ Although petite in size, she loved it! Soon she was attending the sessions regularly, several times a week.

These classes were supposed to be mixed, but Nicola was the only girl there. This didn't bother her at all. She was used to having fist fights with her brothers, after all. 2) _____ She followed exactly the same training programme as the lads in the class, including exchanging punches in the ring. She felt that sparring with the lads would make her a better boxer.

But what was it about boxing that got Nicola so hooked? Whichever way you look at it, getting punched is not a prospect that appeals to a lot of women. 3) _____ She sees boxing as much more than a physical sport. For her, it's a game of the mind, involving willpower and determination. As she sees it, boxers learn dedication, which then carries over into everyday life. If you really put your mind to something, she discovered, you can probably achieve it.

Her dedication to the sport was thoroughly tested when she fell down some stairs and cracked her vertebra on the way to the ring.

Undeterred, she went on to win the match but was so badly injured she couldn't fight for one whole year afterward. 4) _____ Through sheer determination, it seems! And when she returned to boxing, she was better than ever.

5) _____ When she started boxing, public bouts between two women were banned; it was too dangerous, people said, and unfeminine. The ban was finally lifted, for the 2012 Olympic Games, but how would the crowds react to female boxing matches? Given the amount of opposition there had been in the past, would the spectators turn out for the matches? They did, in huge numbers! In fact, the reaction of the spectators was overwhelming, leaving no doubt about the popularity of the event.

It was only after the Games were over that Nicola became aware of the huge inspiration she has been to girls. Her determination to rise above the glass ceiling that had kept women out of a male dominated sport for so long made her a perfect role model for a new generation. The numbers of girls aspiring to follow in her shoes and reach the top in boxing has simply mushroomed. 6) _____ In her opinion, however, equality demands that women be allowed to do any sport they choose. **Whether you agree with her or not, she is definitely an athlete to respect!**

★ ★ ★ ★   ★ ★ ★ ★

VOCABULARY
Keeping fit

1 Choose the word in each list that does not fit in with the others.

1 double fault	foul	~~win~~
2 ace	chalk	knockout
3 spar	champion	opponent
4 umpire	referee	coach
5 dribble	serve	ring
6 net	fist	goalpost
7 pitch	court	punch

2 Complete the text with the best answer, A, B, C or D.

1 A competitor	**B** player	**C** champion	**D** rival
2 A fight	**B** match	**C** play	**D** competition
3 A won	**B** caught	**C** beaten	**D** taken
4 A motivation	**B** expectation	**C** competition	**D** inclination
5 A ring	**B** field	**C** pitch	**D** court
6 A in	**B** below	**C** under	**D** on
7 A dribble	**B** serve	**C** shot	**D** stroke
8 A head	**B** knee	**C** fist	**D** wrist

3 Complete the sentences with these words.

> do   give   have   make
> miss   run   ~~score~~   take

1 The crowd cheered when the local team managed to ___*score*___ a goal.

2 I'm doing my best so please _____ me a break!

3 If you play rugby, you _____ the risk of getting badly injured.

4 The United player was unfortunate enough to _____ a penalty, which meant the team lost the game.

5 If you're a top tennis player, you can _____ a fortune at Wimbledon.

6 Going to dance classes will really _____ you good!

7 If you don't _____ any notice of what the referee says, you'll be sent off the field!

8 To be a champion, you need to _____ a lot of confidence in your skills.

Subject: Andy Murray!

British tennis player Andy Murray waited a long time to win Wimbledon, but in 2013 he finally became 1) ___*champion*___ . In the final 2) _____ , the Championship decider, he'd faced the World Number One, Novak Djokovic. It was an amazing battle, both physically and mentally! Andy had got to the final the previous year too, but had been 3) _____ by Roger Federer. This defeat seemed to have increased his 4) _____ . The British crowd were desperate for him to win and greeted his appearance on 5) _____ with huge applause. After his past failure, he was clearly 6) _____ a lot of pressure to win this time round. Would his nerves destroy his performance? Happily, they didn't. Andy won point after point. Eventually, after nearly three hours of play, he lifted his racket to 7) _____ for the match. The crowd held their breath. Would he win the Championship? He did! Andy punched the air with his 8) _____ as the crowd cheered. There was a male British winner at Wimbledon for the first time in seventy-seven years!

GRAMMAR
Conditionals

1 **Choose the correct form of the verb.**

1 If there *will/would be/are* any tickets left for the match, I'll buy some.

2 If I *wouldn't be/weren't/won't be* so lazy, *I'd go/ I went* for a swim.

3 You'll get fat unless you *take/don't take/will take/ won't take* more exercise.

4 *We go/We'll go* skateboarding tomorrow if the sun *will shine/is shining.*

5 When I *got/get/will get* home, I *look/'ll look* for my tennis racket.

6 Take your camera in case *you'll see/you see/you saw* a celebrity at the arena.

7 If my dad *didn't/wouldn't* work with athletes, I *didn't/wouldn't/don't* meet them so often.

8 I'm not going to the pitch with you unless you *let/ will let* me play.

9 If you *were/would be* offered tickets for a World Cup football match, *would/will* you go?

10 That footballer *never plays/will never play* well unless he *gets/will get* more training.

2 **Cross out the one unnecessary word in each sentence.**

1 Don't bang that racket on the ground in case you will break it.

2 Unless I would play better, the coach will not pick me for the team.

3 We can go out cycling provided if we are back for lunch.

4 Do ring me if you will decide to go to the match.

5 If I would had more money, I would be able to buy more trainers.

6 Take an umbrella in the case it rains.

7 I could go to football practice when I am able to.

8 I could book a court if I would knew how much it costs.

3 **Complete the sentences using the prompts.**

1 If my brother / win / the championship / tomorrow, he may go professional.
If my brother wins the championship tomorrow, he may go professional.

2 We / not / join / the local gym tonight / unless / it / be /cheap.

3 Jan / always / win / when I / play / her at tennis, but I'm hoping to change that soon.

4 They / cancel / the final / if the champion / be / ill, but luckily he was fine.

5 I / take / my football boots with me today in case the trainer / ask me to play. I hope so!

6 I / serve / better in the game last week if I / not injure / my shoulder.

4 **Rewrite the sentences using the words in capitals. Use between two and five words, including the word given.**

1 I don't think you should dive from that rock. WERE
If I *were you, I wouldn't* dive from that rock.

2 She's not getting a new bicycle because she can't afford it.   IF
She would get a new bicycle _____ it.

3 I won't go bowling without you.   UNLESS
I won't go bowling _____ .

4 She played netball because her friend asked her to.   NOT
She wouldn't have played netball if her friend _____ to.

5 Concentrate hard, and you'll win the match.   YOU
You'll win the match if _____ .

6 There's a chance you may fall off your horse, so wear a helmet.   CASE
Wear a helmet _____ your horse.

7 He hurt his leg so he lost the race.   MIGHT
If he hadn't hurt his leg, he _____ the race.

USE OF ENGLISH
Vocabulary: phrasal verbs

1 Choose the correct word.

1 The rugby captain was ill so my brother stood *to/up/in* for him.
2 Most referees won't put up *for/with/by* bad behaviour.
3 Five members of the team have gone *up/down/out* with 'flu!
4 I wish they'd do *in/off/away* with some football rules because I find them confusing.
5 Sadly, our side ran *away with/out of/by from* energy halfway through the game.
6 He scored a goal, which made *in/out/up* for his previous mistake.
7 It's important to get *up/over/on* well with other members of the team.
8 I forgot my football boots today so I had to make do *with/for/to* trainers.
9 Nobody knew how to solve the problem until the coach came *about/up/on* with a brilliant idea.

2 Complete the phrasal verbs (1–8) with these words.

along with   away with   do with   down on
forward to   in for   out of   up with

1 to look forward _____to_____ = to anticipate something with pleasure
2 to look _____ = to treat someone as if they are inferior to you
3 to make _____ = to manage with what you've got
4 to run _____ = to have no more left of something
5 to stand _____ = to replace someone temporarily
6 to go _____ = to agree with an idea or suggestion
7 to do _____ = to get rid of something
8 to put _____ = tolerate a situation or a person

3 Choose the correct answer, A, B or C.

1 You have to _____ with the rules even if you disagree with them.
   A take on
   (B) go along
   C come up
2 Some people criticised the captain, but I _____ up for him.
   A took
   B got
   C stood
3 I think all schools should do _____ all compulsory sport.
   A away with
   B out of
   C along with
4 You shouldn't _____ on somebody just because they're not sporty.
   A bring down
   B come up
   C look down
5 I don't go _____ girls doing boxing.
   A along with
   B in for
   C up with
6 If you haven't got your own boots, you'll have to make _____ these.
   A out with
   B do with
   C up for
7 Our teacher won't put _____ any kind of bad behaviour on the sports field.
   A out from
   B down to
   C up with
8 Oh no! I've got a cut on my foot and we've _____ out of plasters.
   A run
   B gone
   C been
9 He left the team because he didn't get _____ some of the players.
   A up to
   B on with
   C down to
10 I'm looking forward _____ playing in the match on Saturday.
   A in
   B for
   C to

USE OF ENGLISH
Grammar: mixed conditionals

1 Complete the text with an appropriate word in each space. Use any word once only.

Teenage Food Champions

Tanya is 1) _a_ brilliant teenage chef. She 2) _____ be so good at cooking if her dad hadn't fallen ill last year. Her mum works long hours in her job, so there would be nobody to put dinner on the table 3) _____ Tanya hadn't taken over the cooking. There are ready meals waiting in the freezer just in 4) _____ Tanya's efforts end in disaster. But they rarely do! She grows her own salad vegetables, so provided it 5) _____ the right season she has fresh ingredients to use in her food. If she 6) _____ not have much time, she makes pasta or pizza, but she's usually more ambitious than that. She's grateful to her Home Economics teacher. 'If she 7) _____ not helped me, I wouldn't know how to cook for everybody' she says. So is she really a good cook? Take her brother's word for it when he says, 'If I had to to choose between having a dinner cooked by Tanya and going to a fast food restaurant, I 8) _____ choose Tanya's dinner. There's no better recommendation than that!'

2 Complete the sentences by matching the parts.

1 If you didn't eat junk food,
2 If you took more exercise,
3 If you hadn't eaten so many snacks last night,
4 If you had spent less time in the gym,
5 If you hadn't missed the team selection meeting,
6 If you had scored a winning goal,
7 Provided you spend more time training,
8 If you had missed scoring that goal,

a you wouldn't be so popular now.
b you could have made it onto the team.
c you'd be a hero now.
d you wouldn't be so fit now.
e you'd be thinner and healthier.
f you'll reach the top in your sport.
g you could get really fit.
h you might have found it easier to do up your jeans this morning.

3 Choose the correct answer, A, B or C.

1 If I _____ more in the past, I'd be better at tennis now.
   A had practised   **B** practised
   C was practising

2 My sister _____ a ballet dancer if she weren't so tall.
   A could become
   B could be becoming
   C could have become

3 If there weren't a café near our school, we _____ at all yesterday.
   A mightn't have eaten
   B mightn't eat
   C mightn't have been eating

4 If I _____ to the gym more often last year, I'd be fitter now.
   A went   **B** had gone
   C was going

5 If I _____ to bed earlier last night, I'd feel more like taking part in Sports Day today!
   A would have gone   **B** went
   C had gone

6 We wouldn't have to queue now if _____ to book a table in advance.
   A we'd remembered
   B we remembered
   C we'd remember

4 Complete the second sentence so that it means the same as the first.

1 You didn't wash the dishes last night so you have no clean plates this morning.
   But you would _have clean plates this morning if you had washed the dishes last night_ .

2 I can't buy lunch because I left my money at home this morning.
   But if I _____ .

3 I'm only able to cook now because my gran taught me.
   I wouldn't _____ unless _____ .

4 I ate too much so now I'm not able to do up my jeans.
   If I _____ .

5 You're feeling hungry now because you didn't eat breakfast.
   But you _____ .

6 I couldn't meet you earlier because it's my dad's birthday today.
   But if _____ .

LISTENING

1 Read the seven questions in Exercise 2. Which ones are about:

A a speaker's feelings? ....

B a speaker's attitude? ....

C a speaker's purpose? ....

D agreement between speakers? ....

2 🔊 5.1 Listen to seven conversations. Choose the correct answer, A, B or C.

1 You hear two friends talking about a kind of race called a triathlon. What do they agree about the sport?

A It's too demanding physically.

B It's difficult to be good at it.

C It's better for you than other sports.

2 You hear two people talking about diets. How does the girl feel about them?

A concerned about possible harm

B annoyed about the publicity they get

C frustrated about her failure

3 You hear a girl leaving a voicemail message. Why is she calling?

A to confirm an existing arrangement

B to accept an invitation

C to ask a favour

4 You hear two people talking about a new gym. What is the man's attitude?

A He's keen to try it.

B He's sure it will help him get fitter.

C He likes the equipment.

5 You hear an athlete talking about his career. How does he feel about it?

A satisfied with what he has achieved

B proud of the effect he has on others

C relieved that he isn't still competing

6 You hear two people talking about boxing. What do they both think?

A It's a good way to keep fit.

B It needs more regulation.

C Girls should not do it.

7 In this conversation about extreme sports, what is the girl doing?

A explaining why she enjoys them

B describing how it feels to do them

C persuading the man to try them

SPEAKING SKILLS

1 Look at these phrases. What is the speaker doing, A or B?

1 'I get you.'

A showing understanding   **B** disagreeing

2 'Absolutely.'

A clarifying   **B** agreeing

3 'Sorry, you've lost me.'

A asking for clarification   **B** showing understanding

4 'To put it another way,'

A disagreeing   **B** clarifying

5 'I know what you mean.'

A showing understanding   **B** disagreeing

6 'I'm with you now.'

A agreeing   **B** showing understanding

7 'How do you mean?'

A asking for clarification   **B** asking for an opinion

2 Complete the two conversations with these phrases.

> I agree with you that …   In my opinion, …
> I don't understand   Sorry, I'm not with you.
> Let me explain.   Thanks, I'm with you now.

1 **A** I don't think we should do sport during the school day – we have to study. That's more important because we need qualifications for our future.

B 1) _I don't understand_ what you mean – sport's important too, so I don't get your point.

A 2) .... What I mean is, the school day is quite short so we have to make the most of the time and focus on what's important.

B 3) .... it's important to get the balance right, but just working all the time isn't healthy for anyone. Sport is more than just having fun.

A 4) .... it's just a waste of time – sorry.

2 **B** It's really important to develop a competitive spirit in children when they're still at school.

A 5) .... Can you explain?

B Well, the workplace is incredibly competitive and children need to get used to it early otherwise they won't be able to cope with it later on.

A 6) .... But I don't agree, even though I understand what you're saying. Children can get too competitive, and that's not good for them.

WRITING

1 Complete the opinion essay phrases (1–6) with an appropriate word.

1 Let's look at the ___*pros*___ and cons.
2 Some people are against the idea but I'm in _____ of it.
3 _____ for me, I believe the facts speak for themselves.
4 This idea may sound good at first; _____ there are some problems.
5 To my _____, while there are some advantages, I still believe this is a bad idea.
6 There are advantages to the idea but these are outweighed by the _____ .

2 Read the essay and choose the best ending, A or B.

3 Read the essay task. Write 140–190 words in an appropriate style.

> Homework essay title:
> *Should sports that are sometimes dangerous or violent, like boxing or rugby, be banned for both boys and girls?*
>
> Write about:
> • individual choice
> • safety
> • your own view

Should girls be allowed to compete in the same sports as boys?

In our grandparents' time there was a big difference in the ways girls and boys took exercise, both at school and in their free time. People thought boys needed to be strong and tough, so they were taught rough sports like rugby and boxing. Girls, on the other hand, were supposed to be soft and gentle and do more ladylike sports. All this has changed.

These days, women in many countries are fighting for equality with men. They want to be treated in the same way in all aspects of life. When it comes to exercise, many girls have become interested in sports that used to be for boys alone. They enjoy fighting for the ball in rugby, for example, and the mental strength and confidence they get from boxing.

However, although it is clear that some girls enjoy rough sports, there are others who would find them a nightmare. And who can blame them? Not every girl wants to be punched or kicked in the name of sport, or to go around with a black eye or lots of bruises. Boxing can be a very dangerous sport, resulting in serious injury and the same goes for rugby, kick-boxing, and various other sports. In my opinion it is questionable whether these sports should be played by boys, let alone girls!

A In primary school playgrounds, it's usually the little boys who want to fight, while the girls find more constructive ways to spend their time. In my opinion it is not very logical to try and make them act in the same way when they exercise.

B To conclude, I would say that girls should be allowed to do the same sports as boys, but only if that is their choice. Put girls under any pressure, though, and they might be put off sport for life, which would have very bad consequences for their future health and happiness.

Revision Unit 5

1 Choose the correct word.

1 Who's first on the *tennis pitch/ring/court* this morning?
2 If you're competitive, you want to *win/beat/catch* your opponent.
3 The people taking part in a sports event are called *rivals/competitors/champions*.
4 My brother was delighted because he *scored/gained/made* a goal.
5 The footballer was sent off the pitch for committing a *mistake/foul/fault*.
6 The boxer punched the man with his *foot/fist/head*.
7 I'd like to make a pizza, but I haven't got the right *ingredients/menus/foods*.
8 Has she got enough *imagination/intention/motivation* to make her practise night and day to win?

2 Complete the text with one appropriate word in each space. Use any word once only.

Subject: **Sugar Alert!** ⇦ ➡ 🏠

We all know it's important
1) _____to_____ take care of our bodies
2) _____ we want to look good and stay healthy. Playing football or tennis, for example, isn't just great fun; it
3) _____ do you a lot of good, as well. Of course you have to watch your diet, too; 4) _____ you're careful what you eat, you run the risk of becoming overweight or getting ill. If you 5) _____ the wrong kinds of food, you could end up being really moody, too. Why? Because scientists have discovered that sugary foods 6) _____ chocolate and biscuits are 'bad mood foods'. They give you 7) _____ quick burst of energy, but when that wears off, you may feel irritable and tired. So, if you 8) _____ feeling grumpy today, you know what to do – cut out the sugar!

3 Complete the sentences with the correct preposition.

1 David came _____up_____ with a brilliant suggestion for next year's competition.
2 I hope you'll stand _____ for me if the referee blames me for the team's poor performance.
3 We don't really understand why the rules have changed, but we're happy to go _____ with them anyway.
4 Has Paul come _____ from his operation yet or is he still unconscious?
5 Mum says she won't put up _____ us leaving our muddy boots around any more!
6 I'm sorry I let you down, but I promise I'll make up _____ it in another way.
7 The captain comes _____ with some amazing jokes in the changing rooms.
8 I don't get _____ with my trainer at all.

4 Complete the text with the best answer, A, B, C or D.

Daredevils!

Extreme sports usually require a great deal of 1) _skill_ , so the people who 2) ___ part in the activities need to 3) ___ a lot of confidence in themselves. If they don't stay in control of their actions, they run the 4) ___ of hurting themselves really badly. There are no 5) ___ to obey in most of these sports. Participants don't usually join together in 6) ___ either, as they do in football or cricket, for example. Extreme sports can be very dangerous! Street skaters, for example, are always coming 7) ___ with new and even more incredible places to do tricks. If you're interested in extreme sports, I 8) ___ definitely advise you to join a club.

1	A information		**B** skill	
	C knowledge		D duties	
2	A have	B do	C take	D want
3	A contain	B believe	C leave	D have
4	A risk	B opportunity	C hope	D chance
5	A laws	B rules	C commands	D duties
6	A teams	B sides	C lines	D rows
7	A in	B down	C over	D up
8	A will	B shall	C would	D did

5 Complete the words in the sentences.

1 After my main course I had a huge ice cream for
d e s s e r t .

2 I broke my leg so I had to go into hospital for an
o _____ at _____ .

3 Because I hadn't eaten all day I felt very weak
and eventually I f _____ nt _____ .

4 I'm starving hungry! What's on the m _____ u
for dinner tonight?

5 If you're c _____ mp _____ t _____ e, you're
determined to be better than other people.

6 If you have m _____ v _____ t _____ n, you
are keen and willing to do something.

7 You put a s _____ d _____ e on a horse before you
ride it.

8 I'm trying to diet, but I find sugary foods are a
terrible t _____ mp _____ n.

6 Rewrite the words using the sentences in capitals. Use between two and five words, including the word given.

1 My advice is to get more swimming lessons.
YOU
If I _were you, I would get_ more
swimming lessons.

2 I didn't go to the training so I'm not in the
team now.
I
I could be in the team now if _____
the training.

3 He wasn't able to go swimming because he
forgot his swimming things.
COULD
He _____ if he'd remembered his
swimming things.

4 I broke my leg last month so I can't go skiing
this year.
NOT
If I _____ my leg last month, I could go
skiing this year.

5 I'm only asking for extra coaching because I
need it.
UNLESS
I wouldn't ask for extra coaching _____ .

6 You live a long way from green fields so you
can't keep a horse.
NEARER
If _____ to green fields, you could keep
a horse.

7 It might be hot so take some sun cream.
CASE
Take some sun cream _____ hot.

7 Find the mistake in each of these sentences and correct it.

1 If I won't practise tennis every day, I forget how to hit
the ball properly.
If I don't practise tennis every day, I forget
how to hit the ball properly.

2 I'll buy a ticket for the boxing contest, but when I can't
get there in time, you go in without me.

3 You won't be able to play football if you will forget
your boots.

4 I bring your cycle helmet in case you need it, shall I?

5 I'd be careful when doing extreme sports if I'd be you.

6 If I won't see you in the gym, I'll text you.

7 Provided it won't rain tomorrow, we can play the
game outdoors.

8 I won't sell you these trainers unless you don't pay
me immediately.

8 Use the clues to complete the crossword.

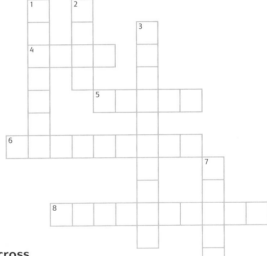

Across

4 You close your hand and make
this if you are going to punch someone.

5 A verb meaning to play in a dishonest way in order
to win

6 An adjective used to describe food that tastes
really good

8 Something you want to have or do even though you
know you should not

Down

1 Someone who makes sure that the rules of a sport
like football are obeyed

2 An adjective to describe food which is prepared
quickly and that you can take away

3 This phrasal verb means *manage with what
you've got.*

7 An adjective to describe food that is very hot and
peppery, like Indian food

06 showtime

READING

1 Complete the sentences using these words. You do not need one of the words.

> auditions   blank   calmly   cue   hitch
> lead   lights   ~~nerve-wracking~~   wings

1 People often find performing on stage a
   _____nerve-wracking_____ experience.

2 An actor knows when to speak because he is given a _____ by another actor.

3 If they want to be cast in a play, actors often have to go to several _____ first.

4 The main acting part in a play or film is called the _____ role.

5 The side of a stage is known as the _____ . and actors wait there to go on stage.

6 If someone 'takes things _____ ', it means they don't get nervous or afraid.

7 If your mind goes _____ in difficult situations, you can't think what you should say.

8 If something goes without a _____ , it goes without any problems.

2 Read the article quickly. Which description best describes it?

A An account of what became a negative experience

B A description of a particularly exciting opportunity

C A discussion about the advantages of being an actor

3 Read the article again. Are the following statements true or false?

1 Actors usually find first night performances easy.
   True   False

2 Connor had always had an ambition to be an actor.
   True   False

3 Connor got involved in Eva's audition by accident.
   True   False

4 The part in the play Connor was given was an unpleasant one.
   True   False

5 The rehearsals for the play went on for six weeks.
   True   False

6 No one came to watch the first performance of the play.
   True   False

4 Choose the best answer, A, B, C or D.

1 Why does Connor mention professional actors at the start of the article?

A to explain the techniques of acting they use

B to compare them with amateur actors

C to show that feeling nervous is normal for them

D to demonstrate how they deal with nerves

2 What does Connor say about the audition he did with Eva?

A It was more enjoyable than he'd expected.

B He had no idea what he was doing.

C It made him feel rather ill.

D He was glad to be of use to a fellow student

3 How did Connor feel about getting the part of the Sherriff of Nottingham?

A He was put off by the number of lines he had.

B He regretted having taken part in the original audition.

C He wished he could have been Robin Hood instead.

D He thought it was a more interesting part than some others.

4 What does the word *this* in line 65 refer to?

A learning how to fight on stage

B the process of memorising lines

C the pressure of the whole thing

D the rehearsals after school

5 What does Connor mean by *butterflies in my stomach* in line 75?

A an excited feeling

B a nervous feeling

C a sick feeling

D a feeling of being upset

6 What do we learn about Connor in the last paragraph?

A He is able to learn from experience.

B He rarely needs help in difficult situations.

C He often has regrets about decisions he's made.

D He finds it difficult to remember things.

A school play

First nights can be nerve-wracking experiences even for professional actors. There is the worry that there hasn't been enough preparation,
5 or that lines apparently firmly secured in the memory, might be forgotten in front of a live audience. It doesn't matter how many times an actor has gone through the experience, fear of
10 the unpredictable can lead to a loss of confidence. So can you imagine how a teenager in his very first play might be feeling, waiting in the wings for his cue to step out onto the stage in front of
15 an auditorium packed with expectant parents, teachers and school mates?

I was fifteen when it happened. I hadn't had any intention of going to
20 the audition, I'd simply been chatting to some mates in the corridor outside the school hall when a teacher, Miss Carter, came out and shouted, 'Connor, you'll do! Eva needs to audition for
25 the play and we need someone to read a part with her. Hurry up!' I tried to get out of it without success. I ended up following Miss Carter into the hall, climbing up onstage and stumbling my
30 way through a scene of Robin Hood. Eva was doing her dramatic best with the part of Maid Marian, the female lead – to be honest, her voice was so loud it nearly gave me a headache.

35 I got through, just, and was about to escape when Miss Carter dragged me back and made me read another scene. I was mystified, but couldn't object.

40 The following day everyone clustered round the notice board to see who was in the play. As I approached everyone turned and stared at me somewhat enviously. Apparently I'd been cast as
45 the Sheriff of Nottingham, which in my opinion was probably the best part in the play. He's deep – he's clever but nasty and has some amusing lines, as opposed to Robin Hood who is just
50 a handsome hero who goes around shooting arrows and getting romantic with Maid Marian. Although I hadn't planned it, surprisingly I wasn't upset.

55 The process of learning lines and rehearsing went on for six weeks, mostly after school, and we all got caught up in the excitement so I didn't notice the pressure building.
60 We were measured for costumes, and shown how to do make-up. After that we were taught how to fight on stage in ways that looked realistic but were actually quite safe,
65 and I found this so enjoyable that it masked other problems I didn't see coming, and possibly paved the way for my downfall.

Suddenly it was almost time for the
70 first performance. I usually take most things fairly calmly and thought this would be no exception. But what did I know? As I was standing backstage and heard all the chattering and rustling
75 from the audience I got butterflies in my stomach. I was quite literally shaking. I knew my family were there expecting me to do well. The house lights went down, the stage lights came on, the
80 music started and the audience fell silent. I watched the first scene from the wings; the audience responded well to a couple of jokes, clapped a few times and then I heard my cue: 'Here's the Sheriff.'
85
My legs wouldn't move, my mind was a complete blank and I was kicking myself for contemplating the idea that I could be a performer. Eva told
90 me later she'd had to push me into the spotlight, and I'd stood there for a few seconds, like a rabbit caught in headlights. I have no memory of being completely dumbstruck – my brain has
95 conveniently erased the moment of humiliation. Apparently Tom repeated my cue, I managed to splutter my first line and the rest of the play went without a hitch. However, it taught me
100 a lesson, which is that I'm not cut out to be an actor. With luck, I'll never stand on a stage again.

VOCABULARY
The arts

1 Choose the correct answer, A, B, C or D.

1 Our school deals very severely with incidents of bullying and _____ .
   - **A** naming
   - **B** labelling
   - **C** nicknaming
   - **(D)** name-calling

2 I can't come out tonight because I've got to learn my _____ for the school play tonight.
   - **A** plays
   - **B** lines
   - **C** notes
   - **D** orders

3 I'd much rather go to a _____ performance of a play than a pre-recorded one.
   - **A** living
   - **B** lively
   - **C** live
   - **D** lifetime

4 To get a part in the musical I had to _____ in front of the director, along with fifty other hopeful actors!
   - **A** rehearse
   - **B** react
   - **C** play
   - **D** audition

5 You need a lot of _____ if you're going to become a lead actor in a film.
   - **A** culture
   - **B** art
   - **C** talent
   - **D** gifts

6 Tom missed two _____ for the play so the director gave his role to someone else.
   - **A** practices
   - **B** meetings
   - **C** acts
   - **D** rehearsals

7 My grandparents _____ so they could get married in secret.
   - **A** departed
   - **B** migrated
   - **C** eloped
   - **D** disobeyed

8 I'll describe the _____ of the film, but I won't give away the ending in case I spoil it for you.
   - **A** plot
   - **B** story
   - **C** event
   - **D** summary

9 Clare wanted the lead role, but she's ended up playing quite a minor _____ instead.
   - **A** person
   - **B** character
   - **C** actor
   - **D** individual

10 My mum has offered to help make the _____ I'll be wearing in the play.
   - **A** robe
   - **B** apparel
   - **C** clothing
   - **D** costume

2 Complete the sentences with these words in the correct form.

> blame   challenge   confess   ~~insult~~   loathe
> mix   quit   struggle

1 Bullies often ___*insult*___ people and call them names.

2 Last week, my best friend _____ me to enter the singing competition.

3 I have always _____ horror films – I just think they're rubbish!

4 The director kept criticising me in rehearsals, so in the end I _____ .

5 Record producers often _____ different sounds together to create a music album.

6 I have a bad memory so I always have to _____ to learn my lines.

7 The director _____ himself when the play did badly at the box office.

8 Jessica _____ last night that she'd stolen some jewellery from the dressing room.

3 Choose the correct answer, A, B or C.

1 Keep quiet about the party because we don't want people to *gate-crash* it!
   - **A** doorstep
   - **B** footpath
   - **(C)** gate-crash

2 When Romeo and Juliet meet, it is a case of love at first _____ .
   - **A** look
   - **B** sight
   - **C** glance

3 Dan's got so many _____ , I think he should see a psychiatrist!
   - **A** hang-ups
   - **B** pin-ups
   - **C** turn-ups

4 In the play, the teenagers get angry and refuse to listen to their parents. Does that _____ any bells with you?
   - **A** sound
   - **B** play
   - **C** ring

5 I'm not sure if Peter will make a good actor, but time will _____ .
   - **A** speak
   - **B** say
   - **C** tell

6 In summer, I often _____ at the beach with my friends.
   - **A** hang up
   - **B** hang out
   - **C** hang down

7 I've had an awful day – everything I've done has gone _____ !
   - **A** wrong
   - **B** bad
   - **C** false

GRAMMAR
Comparative structures

1 Complete the sentences with a comparative or superlative form of the verb in brackets.

1 Jack was *a lot more nervous* than I thought he'd be.
(a lot / nervous)
2 I've just seen the .... rock band in the world. (crazy)
3 The film was .... than I'd expected.
(a great deal / entertaining)
4 Colette is .... dancer in our group.
(by far / talented)
5 I wasn't .... you were. (nearly/good)
6 The more we rehearse the play, the .... I feel about it. (good)
7 This year we have .... free time than normal. (much/little)
8 My singing is .... than yours!
(a great deal / bad)

2 Put the words in the correct order.

1 expensive / us / too / The / were / tickets / for / .
The tickets were too expensive for us.
2 too / were / learn / lines / difficult / for / him / to / The / .
3 ground / enough / sit / The / was / comfortable / to / on / .
4 understand / clever / to / I'm / enough / Shakespeare / not / .
5 stage / high / was / climb / me / to / The / too / for / on / .
6 was / to / pass / I / not / enough / lucky / audition / the / .
7 painting / not / to / enough / good / win / prize / a / The / was / .
8 hard / to / seats / for / sit / were / The / on / too / us / .

3 Correct the mistakes in these sentences.

1 He was very nervous to go on the stage.
He was too nervous to go on the stage.
2 It's too late for to get tickets for the gig.
3 The theatre is too far away that we can walk to.
4 Dad's guitar is too old to play it.
5 Is the ground dry enough to sit?
6 Our director thinks my voice is not enough good.
7 The near we get to the show, the scarier it all seems!
8 We had so a good time at the play!

4 Complete the second sentence so that it means the same as the first.

1 He couldn't wear the crown because it was so heavy.
TOO
The crown was *too heavy for him to* wear.
2 As rock concerts become bigger, they get more exciting.
THE
.... , the more exciting they get.
3 He's too young to be a professional actor.
ENOUGH
He's .... a professional actor.
4 The performance was so good, I'm going to see it again.
SUCH
It was .... I'm going to see it again.
5 Are there any cheaper tickets for the show?
THESE
Are .... for the show?
6 Our music wasn't nearly as loud as yours.
DEAL
Your music was .... ours.
7 The final rehearsal was better than the first performance.
AS
The first performance .... the final rehearsal.
8 I'm not nearly as talented as my friend.
FAR
My friend .... me.

USE OF ENGLISH
Vocabulary: -ght, -th, -ief nouns

1 Choose the correct word.

1 I wanted to act in the play, but I ended *out/off/up* building the set!
2 I arranged to meet a friend at the cinema, but he didn't show *down/round/up*.
3 Our local drama club are hoping to put *up/on/in* a musical this year.
4 Can you hang *on/up/by* a minute while I answer this phone call?
5 Sarah is really bitchy; she's always running people *over/through/down*.
6 If you mess *out/over/around* in class, you'll get into trouble!
7 We need to check *over/by/out* what time the gig starts before we plan our evening.

2 Complete the table below.

	Verb or adjective	Noun
1	fly	*flight*
2	long	
3	think	
4	grieve	
5	see	
6	die	
7	young	
8	weigh	
9	broad	

3 Complete the sentences with the correct form of the word in capitals.

1 Can you guess the _____weight_____ of this crown? It's so heavy to wear! **WEIGH**
2 Katrina is scared to _____ that she'll fall off the stage! **DIE**
3 The guitarist was really nervous, so it was a _____ to hear that the audience were enjoying the concert. **RELIEVE**
4 It must be difficult for actors to portray _____ on the stage. **GRIEVE**
5 Belonging to a dance group is keeping me fit and _____. **HEALTH**

4 Find ten words on the topic of the arts. The words go across, down or diagonally. The first letter of each word is highlighted.

m	j	h	p	x	g	h	w	y	k	z	a	l	p	h
l	a	r	r	e	q	t	t	n	p	b	m	z	x	n
m	w	u	y	o	p	b	p	h	y	d	q	b	y	f
t	t	l	s	n	z	t	i	m	a	k	e	u	p	g
p	a	d	w	v	d	c	x	v	z	e	t	x	z	e
e	s	l	p	r	e	h	e	a	r	s	a	l	q	b
z	e	u	e	d	j	a	e	q	t	t	f	t	e	c
m	t	d	x	n	j	r	j	x	x	f	g	p	z	o
t	k	i	q	o	t	a	u	d	i	t	i	o	n	s
c	p	r	l	q	r	c	u	t	c	c	n	f	m	t
h	i	e	p	l	o	t	d	a	e	u	r	p	j	u
c	b	c	d	f	i	e	w	r	g	i	t	r	s	m
p	p	t	f	p	e	r	f	o	r	m	a	n	c	e
s	o	o	a	w	t	b	b	e	c	o	l	o	g	y
v	z	r	q	q	n	l	s	f	e	j	j	v	z	o

5 Complete the article with the correct form of the words in capitals.

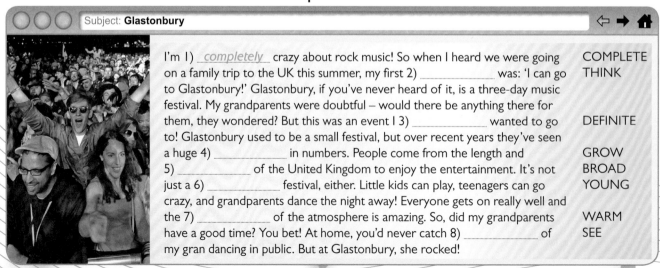

Subject: **Glastonbury**

I'm 1) *completely* crazy about rock music! So when I heard we were going on a family trip to the UK this summer, my first 2) _____ was: 'I can go to Glastonbury!' Glastonbury, if you've never heard of it, is a three-day music festival. My grandparents were doubtful – would there be anything there for them, they wondered? But this was an event I 3) _____ wanted to go to! Glastonbury used to be a small festival, but over recent years they've seen a huge 4) _____ in numbers. People come from the length and 5) _____ of the United Kingdom to enjoy the entertainment. It's not just a 6) _____ festival, either. Little kids can play, teenagers can go crazy, and grandparents dance the night away! Everyone gets on really well and the 7) _____ of the atmosphere is amazing. So, did my grandparents have a good time? You bet! At home, you'd never catch 8) _____ of my gran dancing in public. But at Glastonbury, she rocked!

COMPLETE
THINK

DEFINITE

GROW
BROAD
YOUNG

WARM
SEE

USE OF ENGLISH
Grammar: articles

1 Complete the table by putting the nouns in the correct list.

> actor   album   ~~documentary~~   growth
> happiness   idea   love   music
> people   pride   programme   success

Countable nouns	Uncountable nouns
1 *documentary*	1
2	2
3	3
4	4
5	5
6	6

2 Complete the sentences with *a/an*, *the*, or -.

1 I really enjoyed ____*the*____ documentary about stage schools last night.
2 The producer was amazed at _____ success of the latest vampire movie.
3 I'm getting _____ car next year – Dad's promised me his old one!
4 The theme of the ballet is '_____ love in the time of war'.
5 The show was held to award _____ people who work behind the scenes in the theatre.
6 My all-time favourite single is *Money Can't Buy You* _____ *Happiness* by Jesse J.
7 _____ YouTube clip is a great way to show friends what you've been doing.
8 Alex was _____ homeless and busking on the streets when he was offered a recording contract.
9 I think _____ health is more important than fame.
10 Shakespeare's plays belong to _____ world, not to just one country.
11 I felt a strong sense of _____ pride when my sister came on stage.
12 How did you come up with _____ idea for the musical? It's so original!

3 Correct the mistakes in each of these sentences.

1 The health is an important concern for any actor.
   Health is an important concern for any actor.
2 Without the love, the world would be a sad place.
3 I think my dad will have to buy the new car in a year or two.
4 French are excellent cooks.
5 Did you see a documentary they showed at 6 p.m. yesterday on the Discovery Channel?
6 You need the intelligence to be a great playwright like Shakespeare!
7 There's been huge growth in numbers of people using YouTube.
8 My brother's success has brought him the enormous happiness.

4 Complete the text by adding *a/an*, *the* or – in the gaps.

A Day in … Life of … Dancer

Oliver Carter is 1) ___*a*___ member of 2) _____ famous ballet company and is currently playing 3) _____ lead role as Romeo, in the ballet 'Romeo and Juliet'. Today, like 4) _____ most days in Oliver's life, is very busy. He starts with 5) _____ general practice classes; these follow 6) _____ same routine every day. After class, there's time for 7) _____ short break. Oliver and his friends find 8) _____ spare studio, put on 9) _____ music, and imagine they're dancing in 10) _____ club. They try out 11) _____ steps and tricks. If somebody has 12) _____ idea for a cool new step, 13) _____ others have a go at it, too. After 14) _____ break, it's back to serious business. First he has 15) _____ rehearsals to go to, then it's time for 16) _____ evening show. It's a busy life, but Oliver takes 17) _____ great pride in his dancing and is delighted with 18) _____ success he's had so far. For him, he says, 19) _____ life without dance would be unbearable.

LISTENING

1 ◀ 6.1 **Listen and match the speakers (1–5) with the events (A-E) that they describe.**

Speaker 1   **A**   ballet
Speaker 2   **B**   outdoor rock festival
Speaker 3   **C**   live musical
Speaker 4   **D**   choir recital
Speaker 5   **E**   reality show

2 ◀ 6.2 **Listen again. Match each speaker (1-5) with the correct information (a–h). You do not need three of the letters.**

Speaker 1   _h_
Speaker 2   ....
Speaker 3   ....
Speaker 4   ....
Speaker 5   ....

a   helped another person at the event.
b   met some celebrities after the event.
c   enjoyed the event more than expected.
d   felt the event was not well organised.
e   was annoyed by another person's actions.
f   lost something important at the event.
g   wonders whether she made the right choice of event.
h   was a little disappointed by the event.

SPEAKING SKILLS

1 **Look at the photos and complete the sentences with these words. You do not need one of the words.**

> busking   trumpet   drum   feeling   imagine
> instruments   look   more   playing
> singing   whereas

1 In Photo 1, the people in the foreground are ....

2 In Photo 1, the man between the two guitarists is playing a kind of ....

3 In Photo 1, there are two guys .... the guitar and ....

4 I .... the buskers are excited, and maybe a bit nervous too.

5 In Photo 2, the boys .... as if they're in a school orchestra.

6 In Photo 2, the boys are playing various brass .... such as the ....

7 In Photo 1, the buskers are playing to passers-by, ... the boys in Photo 2 are playing to people who've come to hear their music.

8 The orchestra in Photo 2 is much .... formal than the street band in Photo 1.

2 **Complete these sentences from a discussion.**

1 ......_In_...... my opinion, it's a good idea because …

2 What do you think .... giving money to buskers?

3 I see .... you mean.

4 But perhaps it depends .... how good they are.

5 .... you say, they do need to be reasonably good!

WRITING

1 Choose the correct answer, A, B or C.

What is the main purpose of a review?

A to describe something

B to help the reader make a choice about something

C to provide factual information about something

2 Choose the two correct answers.

Which two of the following do review writers not normally do?

A give his/her own opinion about something

B try to catch the reader's interest

C use interesting vocabulary

D use bullet points

E give very detailed information about the subject of the review

F include negative opinions about the subject of the review

G use rhetorical questions

3 Put these things in the order in which they usually occur in a review.

A The reviewer's recommendations

B Brief details of the subject of the review

C The reviewer's own opinion of the subject

4 Choose the correct answers.

1 It's a great film that I can *well/thoroughly* recommend.

2 I *strongly/loudly* suggest you try to get a ticket for this film!

3 My advice is to give this film a *miss/loss* – it's not worth the money.

4 If you go to see this film you won't *complain/regret* it – you'll have a lot of fun.

5 The acting in this film is *absolutely/very* fantastic.

6 The special effects are *very/simply* amazing.

7 My opinion of this film is that it's rather disappointing – in fact, it's a real *let-down/let-up*.

8 You *wouldn't/shouldn't* miss this film – it's very special.

5 Read the task, then answer the question below.

You see this announcement in your school magazine.

Reviews needed!

Have you seen a television programme that you really enjoyed?

Write us a review of the programme, explaining what the programme was about, and why it was so enjoyable. Say whether you would recommend this programme to other people, and why.

Write 140-190 words

Which is the best introduction for the review, A, B or C?

A One programme that is quite good on television is called *This Week*. I enjoy it.

B I don't watch very much television normally, but one programme did catch my attention when I read about it – it's called *Every Man*. It's advertised as an exciting, fast-moving and thrilling series.

C I don't like watching television, but one programme that isn't bad is called *Country Living*. It's about a family living in the country.

6 Put the paragraphs A, B and C in the best order (1–3) for the rest of the review. Look at Exercise 3 again to help you.

A I recommend this to anyone who enjoys thrillers, although if you prefer romance you might want to give it a miss!

B The programme is about a man who is trying to find his family who he thought had been killed several years before. He follows clue after clue, and finds there is more to the situation than he thought.

C I find it very engaging. The acting is excellent, and the locations are beautiful. The story is well-written, and each episode leaves you wanting to know more.

7 Write your answer to the question below in 140–190 words, using an appropriate style.

REVIEWS WANTED!
What books do you like? We want to know! Send us a review of your favourite book.

Revision Unit 6

1 Choose the correct word.

1 Our youth club is planning to put *up/on/over* a concert.

2 What I enjoy most in my free time is listening to *music/the music/a music*.

3 A good friend should support you, not run you *up/out/down*.

4 Many people enjoy watching *the/-/a* good soap opera.

5 I'm sure there's no such thing as love *from/at/in* first sight.

6 I love *Italian/the Italian/an Italian* food.

7 She thinks she's in love but time will *say/speak/tell*!

8 That comedy film is *such/so/such a* funny!

9 Please hurry up and stop messing *around/up/on*!

10 *The/-/A* good friend is the most important thing you can have.

2 Complete the words in the sentences.

1 A d *i r e c t o* r is the person who is in charge of a play or film and tells actors what to do.

2 The events that form the main story of a play or film are called the p _____ t.

3 An occasion when someone entertains people with a play or a piece of music is called a p _____ f _____ c _____ .

4 A person in a book, play, film, etc is a ch _____ c _____ r.

5 People who listen to or watch a performance are called the au _____ ce.

6 A short performance by an actor to see if he or she is good enough for a part is called an au _____ io _____ .

7 The clothes worn on stage by an actor are called a c _____ s _____ e.

8 The time when all the people in a play practise before the performance is called a r _____ h _____ s _____ l.

3 Complete the sentences with the correct form of the words in capitals.

1 Actors need to be ___*healthy*___ people. HEALTH

2 The _____ of getting up on stage and performing really scares me! THINK

3 We wanted to see the show but it was _____ to get tickets. POSSIBLE

4 My mum likes watching documentaries about _____ issues. SOCIETY

5 What is the _____ of the stage? WIDE

6 Are you coming to _____ club tonight? YOUNG

7 Sonya's got a _____ to make to you! CONFESS

8 I'm _____ going to be a rock singer one day soon! DEFINITE

4 Choose the correct answer, A, B or C.

1 The artist put a lot of _____ into his painting.
   A the love   **(B)** love   C a love

2 The members of the band are _____ nice people.
   A so   B such a   C such

3 We wish you lots of _____ in the future!
   A happiness
   B a happiness
   C the happiness

4 I think _____ should contribute more money to the arts.
   A rich   B the rich   C a rich

5 Pamela's off to _____ for three years to study drama.
   A university   B the university   C an university

6 Do you know who invented _____ ?
   A a car   B car   C the car

7 There was a good programme about _____ on TV last night.
   A the gorillas   B gorillas   C any gorillas

8 _____ advertisement on YouTube can bring in a lot of money, but this one didn't.
   A An   B Some   C The

5 Complete the text with one appropriate word in each space. Use any word once only.

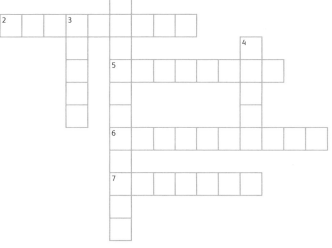

○○○ Confessions of a teen soap addict ⇦ ➡ 🏠

My mum adores soap operas. If she didn't, I might never have become 1) ___*as*___ addicted as I am now. The more unlikely the storylines are, 2) _____ more she enjoys them. Personally, I like watching teen soaps far 3) _____ than adult ones, because they explore interesting teen problems, especially boy-girl relationships. You know the kind of chat that goes on: 'But prove that you love me more 4) _____ anything in the world!' or 'I've just met the 5) _____ gorgeous person in the world – but how do I get 6) _____ date?' Watching soaps is not just a waste of time, though – at least I don't think it is. I know a 7) _____ deal more about relationships now, for a start. And I'm a lot 8) _____ worried about dating new people – in fact, I'm quite relaxed about it now. But is that because I watch soaps or not? What do *you* think?

6 Rewrite the sentences using the words in capitals. Use between two and five words, including the word given.

1 There's no better musical in the theatre.
THE
This ___*is the best musical*___ in the theatre.

2 He spoke more slowly than anyone.
AS
Nobody spoke _____.

3 The girls weren't as nervous as the boys.
LESS
The girls _____ the boys.

4 Each time I listen to that music I like it more.
I
The _____ that music, the more I like it.

5 How long is the stage?
THE
What _____ the stage?

6 I'm amazed at how strong he is.
HIS
I'm amazed _____.

7 Complete the text with the best answer, A, B, C or D.

The Call of the Stage!

When I was just thirteen, my best friend 1) *challenged* me to compete in a talent show. I won, and it was 2) _____ best feeling in the world! Later, I joined a theatre group. They were busy 3) _____ on a musical – and I got the lead role. I was really nervous at the first 4) _____. But the other actors were very friendly and I enjoyed 5) _____ out with them during breaks. I had to learn my lines off by 6) _____ of course – and my songs, too. On the opening night, I was scared – I thought everything might 7) _____ wrong. It didn't, thank goodness, and the play was 8) _____ success.

1 Ⓐ challenged B bet C insisted D admitted
2 A a B some C just D the
3 A getting B putting C bringing D taking
4 A meetings B trials C rehearsals D practices
5 A hanging B sitting C relaxing D being
6 A memory B brain C heart D ear
7 A end B come C finish D go
8 A the B some C a D one

8 Use the clues to complete the crossword.

Across
2 To go to a party that you have not been invited to
5 To try very hard to achieve something difficult
6 An idiom that means to learn all of a piece of writing from memory
7 A phrasal verb that means 'criticise someone unkindly'

Down
1 A quick, intensive course
3 To leave home secretly to get married
4 To say somebody is responsible for something bad

07 School matters

READING

1 **Read the article and choose the correct answer, True or False.**

1 Students knew that their school was going to be filmed for a long time in advance.
True   (False)

2 Cameras picked out boys fighting in the courtyard.
True   False

3 The fence had a negative effect on student behaviour.
True   False

4 Some students were forced to carry other students' property.
True   False

5 It's harder to steal now that every student has a smart card.
True   False

6 Students were less likely to damage and break things after the changes.
True   False

2 **Read the article. Match the questions (1–9) with the paragraphs (A–E).**

Which paragraph mentions:

1 neglecting to do something required by those in charge? C

2 inviting a range of people to find answers to difficulties? ....

3 giving the impression of being in a different kind of institution? ....

4 reacting quickly to a particular signal? ....

5 being influenced by an experience to study a particular subject? ....

6 doing something risky that required courage? ....

7 being uncertain about how to react to a particular event? ....

8 causing damage to places used to store items? ....

9 taking steps to make it more difficult for people to steal? ....

SCHOOL ON TV

A How would you feel if a team of cameramen arrived at your school and started filming you and your friends for national TV? Would you be delighted or worried? My brother felt a mixture of both when, at the very last minute, he and the other students heard their school had been chosen for a 'fly on the wall' documentary series. Having a hidden camera pick up your behaviour, which is what this kind of programme involves, could land students who misbehave in big trouble! My brother's school is a tough, inner-city comprehensive with quite a few discipline problems; letting the cameras in was a brave decision!

B The first programme started with morning break. It was chaos – like rush hour on the Tube! When the bell rang, students started rushing along the narrow corridors and out into a sunless courtyard. Teachers patrolled up and down, stepping in quickly when a fight broke out. 'When students bully each other or fight, it usually takes place in a corridor,' one teacher told viewers. Meanwhile, out in the courtyard, boys were kicking a ball to each other or playing similar games. They took up most of the space in the courtyard so the poor girls were confined to the edges, with little room to move. 'It makes us feel we're not important,' some girls complained. At the far end of the courtyard was a high fence. Its purpose was to protect students, but it made the place look and feel like a prison. This made the students want to rebel against authority.

C Discipline was not the only problem though. As the students marched back to their classrooms at the end of break, many were loaded up with coats, bags, books, and even PE kit. Didn't they have lockers where they could leave their property safely during the day? 'We've given up using lockers because they keep getting vandalised,' one student explained. 'People steal from them too.' Apparently, some kids had got so tired of carrying heavy stuff round that they often didn't even bring heavy books to school any more. And that meant trouble with their teachers.

D All was clearly not well at the school – but help was at hand. The purpose of the documentary was to show how redesigning a school building can improve how students behave and how well they do in school. Viewers saw architects, staff and students coming together to discuss problems and devise solutions. The first change they made was to put a permanent reception desk just inside the entrance, with a receptionist checking who came in and out of the building. This removed the need for high fences. A system of smart cards was also introduced; students could use these to get into the rooms and areas they were allowed to enter, and also to open their new lockers which had now been placed in a brightly lit area. The cards could be used to check belongings in and out of school too, which reduced the incidence of theft.

E All these changes took place during a break in filming. When the cameras returned to the school six months later, the results were amazing. Students felt a million times more positive about their environment and there were far fewer acts of vandalism, truancy, and bullying in the schools. And my brother? He's enjoyed being on TV so much he's decided to study drama!

VOCABULARY
Education

1 Choose the correct words.

1 The boxer's _knuckles_/ankles were red because he'd been punching so hard.

2 My teacher is very _disciplined_/strict with us if we misbehave.

3 We're not allowed to run in any of the _corridors_/alleys in our school.

4 I had to stay after school for detention as a _correction_/punishment for missing class.

5 When Mum married Dad she kept her own _surname_/nickname instead of taking his.

6 If you want a teacher, you need to knock on the door of the _personnel_/staff room.

7 The class bully has been _expelled_/excluded for two weeks.

8 I prefer to learn at my own _grade_/pace.

2 Complete the sentences with these words.

~~forum~~ method pace punishment
row subject torture victim

1 Last night I gave my views in an online _forum_ about modernising school buildings.

2 Mathematics used to be my worst _____ at school.

3 I think it's better if teachers let you learn at your own _____ .

4 I had to stay after school for detention as a _____ for missing class.

5 If you're a _____ of bullying, it's important that you tell an adult.

6 We sat in the back _____ of the cinema.

7 In my little sister's school, they've introduced a new _____ of teaching reading.

8 Studying for exams in summer is pure _____ .

3 Complete the words in the sentences.

1 I got into trouble at school so I was given de _t_ _e_ _n_ _t_ ion.

2 The classroom b _____ y tried to order me around today.

3 We did a really interesting exp _____ t in our science class today.

4 The new school t _____ m starts on September 15th.

5 I'm going to have a private t _____ r to help me with my maths.

6 My favourite s _____ c ____ s are English and history.

7 My parents put me in a bo _____ d _____ g school, so I only went home for the holidays.

8 If you want to be a school pr ____ f _____ , you have to be a good leader.

9 Our teachers get angry if we don't p ____ r _____ p _____ in class.

10 My real name is Pamela, but my n _____ kn _____ is Poppy.

4 Complete the sentences with _make_ or _do_ in the correct form.

1 Oh no! I _have made_ a huge mistake in my test and it's too late to correct it.

2 My mum says she just can't _____ without a dishwasher.

3 Don't _____ Paul laugh! He's trying to concentrate.

4 When Lucia hears that you've stolen her boyfriend, it'll _____ her cry.

5 _____ me a favour and lend me your phone, will you?

6 Tim _____ his best in the test today, but he doesn't think he's passed.

7 I'm hopeless at _____ decisions!

8 We _____ an experiment in class and the test tube exploded!

GRAMMAR
The passive

1 Complete the sentences with the missing word.

1 Has your mobile phone _____*been*_____ found yet?
2 You won't _____ allowed to wear that to school!
3 It's not fair! Our teachers _____ us do so much homework!
4 My sister's not _____ to have a tattoo. My parents have forbidden it.
5 I _____ never been punished for cheating.
6 The best students _____ given prizes in the ceremony yesterday.
7 I hope I _____ not be asked to read my essay out loud in class tomorrow.
8 By the time I got to the school party, all the cakes _____ been eaten!

2 Complete the sentences with the correct form of the verb in brackets.

1 The exam results _*were announced*_ (announce) yesterday.
2 We _____ (not/allow) to take mobile phones into class. It's against the school rules.
3 At this very moment my brother _____ for a place at university. (interview)
4 In our school, cheating _____ (punish) very severely.
5 Our new sports block _____ (open) by a celebrity next week.
6 We had to study in the café while our classroom _____. (redecorate)
7 By the time the fire engine arrived, the fire in the science lab _____. (put out)
8 _____ of the date of the trip by the school yet? (you/inform)

3 Complete the second sentence so that it means the same as the first.

1 They gave the student a warning about her behaviour.
   The student _*was given a warning about her behaviour*_ .
2 They are demolishing the old gymnasium.
   The old gymnasium _____ .
3 They don't let students leave the school at lunchtime.
   Students _____ .
4 Has anyone told the teacher what happened?
   Has the _____ ?
5 Someone is telling my friend off at this minute.
   My friend _____ .
6 They made us all stay in school for detention.
   We _____ .
7 Is anyone taking care of the visitors?
   Are _____ ?
8 They will appoint a new member of staff next term.
   A new member of staff _____ .

4 Put the words in the correct order.

1 students / made / write / to / The / were / lines / .
   The students were made to write lines.
2 been / not / the / Has / cleaned / yet / classroom / ?
   _____
3 flowers / given / teacher / was / The / .
   _____
4 How / cook / taught / to / were / you / ?
   _____
5 spend / was / Each / ten dollars / spend / given / to / student / .
   _____
6 been / repaired / yet / computer / the / Has / ?
   _____
7 allowed / to / We / jeans / not / are / wear / school / in / .
   _____
8 post / results / Will / sent / in / our / be / exam / the / ?
   _____

USE OF ENGLISH
Vocabulary: words with similar meanings

1 Choose the correct answer, A, B, C or D.

1 I was shocked at the .... remarks the bully made.

A vicious   **B** hard   **C** violent   **D** tough

2 The boys who painted graffiti on the school walls are complete ....

A gangs   **B** bullies   **C** torturers   **D** vandals

3 Our teacher encouraged us all to .... in the drama class.

A include   **B** participate   **C** take   **D** enjoy

4 I think they should .... school uniforms all round the world.

A abolish   **B** exclude   **C** expel   **D** abandon

5 You'll get punished if you disobey the school ....

A laws   **B** rules   **C** orders   **D** rulers

6 What .... did you get in your exam?

A notes   **B** remarks   **C** numbers   **D** grades

2 Complete the sentences with these words.

> detect   distance learning   hand   ~~online~~
> rules   state of the art   step   take

1 Part of our coursework involves doing ...*online*... research.

2 Next year I have to .... exams to get into medical school.

3 Examiners can .... cheats by checking on exam candidates' handwriting.

4 We're not allowed to type the essay – we've got to write it out by ....

5 They threw him out of the gang because he wouldn't follow their ....

6 You've helped me a lot, but could you go one .... further and type this out for me?

7 We've got a brand new, ... gym in our school.

8 If you live too far from a university to go there regularly, you can study by .... instead.

3 Choose the correct answer.

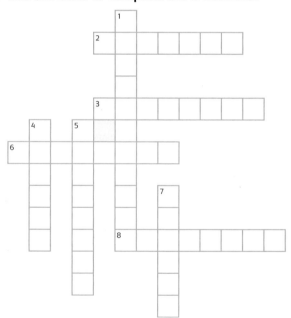

View previous comments   Cancel Share Post

I've been participating in an 1) *outline*/*online* forum about examinations. We've been discussing whether we'd prefer to 2) *take*/*make* one big, end-of-year exam, or be tested regularly during each school 3) *period*/*term*. I don't get stressed by exams and I usually get good 4) *notes*/*grades*, so exams aren't a problem for me. But I know other students who consider them 5) *torture*/*injury* and would be really happy if exams were 6) *excluded*/*abolished* for good. The problem with continuous tests or assessment is that it's not difficult for students to 7) *fault*/*cheat*. If this coursework is written out by hand, examiners can easily 8) *tell*/*detect* cheating. But these days most students type their coursework. So are final exams fairer? What do *you* think?

Write a comment   Support

4 Use the clues to complete the crossword.

Across

2 People who deliberately damage things

3 A short or friendly name given to you by friends and family

6 To destroy a building completely

8 To be forbidden to come to school for a period of time

Down

1 A verb meaning *take part in*

4 A verb meaning *to notice something that is not easy to see*

5 A long passageway in a school

7 Someone who has been attacked

USE OF ENGLISH
Grammar: more passive forms

1 Rewrite the sentences using the words in capitals. Use between two and five words, including the word given.

1 They were always punishing James.   GETTING
   James was always getting punished.

2 They forced me to have extra violin lessons. MADE
   I _____ extra violin lessons.

3 Teachers were planning the new timetable.
                                                    PLANNED
   The new timetable _____ teachers.

4 They won't let us study outdoors.   ALLOWED
   We _____ outdoors.

5 That printer needs repairing.   SHOULD
   That printer _____.

6 Are they still making CDs these days?   MADE
   Are CDs _____ these days?

2 Choose the correct answer, A, B or C.

1 Our classroom needs to _____.
   A redecorate
   B being redecorated
   C be redecorated

2 Do you agree that uniforms _____?
   A they should be banned
   B should ban
   C should be banned

3 My sister _____ me to help her with her homework.
   A got
   B had
   C made

4 Cheats ought _____.
   A to punish
   B to be punished
   C to be punishing

5 The playground should _____ by now.
   A it be reopened
   B being reopened
   C be reopened

6 That printer needs _____.
   A to repair
   B repairing
   C to have repaired

3 Complete the sentences with *have*, *get* or *need* in an appropriate form and a verb from the box.

| clean | ~~have cut~~ | take out | wash |

 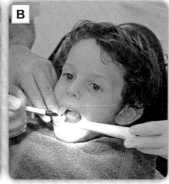

1 My sister *is having* her hair *cut* today.

2 Tom _____ a tooth _____ yesterday.

3 My dad _____ me _____ his car.

4 Those windows _____!

4 Complete the sentences with an appropriate form of the verb in brackets.

1 Dad's got to *get the car serviced*. (get/the car/service)

2 _____ like I asked you? (get/those notes/type)

3 Oh no! I _____. (have/my phone/steal)

4 There's something wrong with your bicycle. It _____. (need/check)

5 You can _____ if you're brave enough. (get/yourself/tattoo)

6 I wear glasses and I need to _____ every two years. (have/my eyes/test)

7 Did you make this mess? _____ now! (Get/it/tidy)

8 Excuse me! Can I _____ here? (get/my photos/enlarge)

LISTENING

1 Complete the sentences with the correct form of the words in brackets.

1 I was ___secretly___ (secret) happy about the trip.
2 The trip was an _____ (excite) prospect for me.
3 There are lots of _____ (formal) to go through at an airport.
4 Having lessons _____ (complete) in English was quite hard.
5 Evening activities were _____ (option) so we didn't have to do them.
6 I'm _____ (passion) about music – I love it so much.
7 I _____ (particular) like trying different types of food.
8 I _____ (actual) enjoyed the course more than I'd expected.

2 🔊 **7.1 Listen to Xavier making a presentation to his class about taking a short language course in England. Complete the sentences with a word or short phrase from the presentation.**

1 Xavier went on the language course that his ___teacher___ said would be right for him.
2 Xavier said he felt _____ when he started his journey to England.
3 Xavier uses the word _____ to describe the distance from the plane to passport control at Heathrow airport.
4 Xavier was pleased he had contacted his host family through _____ before he arrived in England.
5 Xavier made friends with a boy at the school because _____ was an interest they shared.
6 According to Xavier, the English lessons were never _____ although they were long.
7 The evening activity Xavier liked best was going to the _____ for the first time.
8 When Xavier's host family took him out for the day, he enjoyed spending time at the _____ most.
9 Xavier recommends that people going to England take _____ with them.
10 Xavier preferred the _____ to other English food that he tried.

SPEAKING SKILLS

1 Read the discussion task and the five points (A–E) to consider.

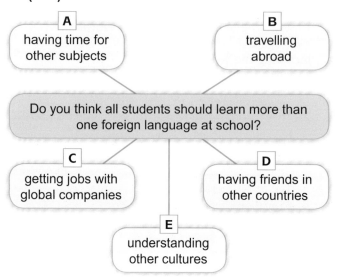

A having time for other subjects

B travelling abroad

Do you think all students should learn more than one foreign language at school?

C getting jobs with global companies

D having friends in other countries

E understanding other cultures

Which of these statements is true, A, B or C?

A You should discuss what makes it difficult to learn a language
B You should discuss different ways of learning a language
C You should discuss whether it's a good idea to learn more than one language

2 Match the ideas (1–5) with the five points in the discussion task, (A–E).

1 having holidays, speaking to local people, understanding menus ___B___
2 finding it difficult, spending too long learning vocabulary, enjoying other subjects _____
3 watching foreign films, visiting interesting places, eating different food _____
4 using social media, writing to pen friends, visiting friends _____
5 working abroad, getting promotion, working with colleagues _____

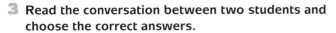

3 Read the conversation between two students and choose the correct answers.

A I think everyone should learn more than one language at school. After all, we live in a global world, *don't we/do we*?

B That's true, but there are more important subjects to study, like maths, *aren't there/isn't it*? Maths takes a lot of time to learn, too.

A I'm not sure. Let's think about that, *will we/shall we*? We can use calculators if we need to, but we can't make a computer speak for us. That doesn't make maths more important, *does it/doesn't it*?

B You may be right – and I agree that everyone wants to travel abroad nowadays, *does he/do they*? It's very popular.

A Yes, for both work and holidays! I certainly want to work for a global company in future, and I guess that would be impossible if I couldn't speak different languages, *isn't it/wouldn't it*? Plus a holiday is much more fun if you can speak to people who live there.

B I agree with you – it's not very nice if you can't understand what a menu says, *can you/is it*? You could make a big mistake with what you ordered!

A It certainly could spoil a holiday, *couldn't it/wouldn't it*?

4 The students had to answer the question 'Which is the most important reason for students to learn more than one language at school?' Choose two things they should do in their discussion.

a Repeat ideas they've already discussed in the task

b Consider how important each reason really is

c Suggest new reasons for learning more than one language

d Agree on the most important reason for learning more than one language

5 Which of these phrases are used for making a suggestion (S) or for reaching a decision (D)?

1 I think this one might be good. ....S........

2 Let's decide on this one. ....

3 How about this one? ....

4 Do you think we should choose this one? ....

5 Let's agree on this one. ....

6 This is definitely the best. ....

WRITING

1 Read the task and put the sentences from an opening paragraph in the correct order (1–4).

> **Articles wanted**
>
> Write an article describing the best teacher you've ever had and explaining why the methods he/she used helped you to learn.

a .... But when they do, they can really change your life!

b .... If you have, you're very lucky; teachers like this don't come along every day.

c .... And have you experienced teaching that is so interesting, exciting, or fun that you couldn't wait for the next class?

d .... Have you ever had a teacher who really brought a subject alive for you?

2 Underline the topic sentence in this paragraph.

I'm speaking from experience. You see, my new literature teacher has turned a subject I had previously found boring into my absolute favourite. I'm even planning to study it at university – if I get good grades. And believe it or not, I think I will!

3 Match the extracts from an article (1–4) with the rhetorical features (a–d).

1 Now please don't get me wrong – this didn't happen overnight.

2 When Mr Turner took over our class mid-term, we were a bunch of savages – no teacher was safe in our hands!

3 There was a reason for this: although our former teacher knew his subject well, his lessons were predictable. First he'd make us copy from the board and then he'd just talk while we took notes. We were bored – which is why we rebelled. And when Mr Turner took over, we expected the same.

4 Who could have guessed that our new teacher would revolutionise our learning?

    a rhetorical question

    b humour

    c good range of connectors

    d direct address to the reader

4 Write your own answer to the task in 140–190 words, using an appropriate style.

Revision Unit 7

1 Choose the correct answer, A, B, C or D.

1 The content of that bully's email was really _____ .
   (A) vicious **B** strict **C** violent **D** passive
2 Love is the main _____ of the book I'm reading.
   A area **B** theme **C** part **D** plot
3 Who was _____ for breaking the glass?
   A guilty **B** blaming
   C responsible **D** embarrassed
4 Football _____ covered the walls in graffiti.
   A gangs **B** bullies **C** victims **D** vandals
5 Before I write my essay, I need to do a lot of _____ into the subject.
   A research **B** study
   C study **D** searching
6 I really like the first _____ of that story.
   A row **B** line **C** speech **D** subject
7 Why don't you type that instead of writing it all out _____ hand?
   A by **B** from **C** with **D** in
8 The teacher wasn't _____ that Sally was cheating.
   A awake **B** known **C** alert **D** aware

2 Complete the sentences with these words.

detect   exclude   grade   ~~pace~~   participate   row   strict   term

1 I don't want to hurry this; I'd prefer to work at a steady ____*pace*____ .
2 Examiners are always trying to _____ if we're cheating.
3 They're planning to _____ Emma for bullying another girl.
4 The drama teacher makes us _____ in all the activities.
5 What _____ did you get in the exam?
6 If we hurry, we can sit in the back _____ of the lecture room.
7 I wish the headteacher wasn't always so _____ .
8 I can't believe it's the last day of _____ tomorrow!

3 Read the blog and choose the best answer, A, B, C or D.

View previous comments   Cancel   Share   Post

If I were a teacher for just one day, I'd cut the length of the school 1) _*term*_ so that students had longer holidays. I'd rewrite all those boring school 2) _____ about what students can and cannot do – like text friends in class. Next, I'd get the 3) _____ changed so that the most boring 4) _____ are dropped for good. I wouldn't be a pushover, but I wouldn't be too 5) _____ , either. Of course, I wouldn't 6) _____ my students wear a uniform. I'd 7) _____ them dress exactly how they like. Oh, and I'd 8) _____ single-sex schools, too. So, would I make a good teacher? What do *you* think?

Write a comment   Support

	A		B		C		D	
1	day		period		row		**(D)** term
2	rules		laws		orders		lines
3	diary		calendar		timetable		routine
4	themes		subjects		topics		areas
5	strict		rough		laid-back		patient
6	force		control		require		make
7	free		enable		let		allow
8	expel		abolish		punish		exclude

4 Find ten words on the topic of schools and education. The words go across, down or diagonally. The first letter of each word is highlighted.

a	t	h	o	m	e	w	o	r	k	d	b	o
x	h	j	q	a	d	w	z	e	t	e	d	z
c	o	r	r	i	d	o	r	j	y	t	s	x
c	e	s	e	e	p	n	y	x	h	e	g	s
l	u	s	e	n	x	r	t	l	p	n	l	y
a	s	u	x	n	h	c	e	a	v	t	i	g
s	t	b	p	u	a	f	l	n	d	i	o	r
s	r	j	e	u	a	p	d	u	t	o	e	a
r	i	e	l	w	b	b	q	z	d	n	f	d
o	c	c	l	a	m	h	j	y	i	e	c	e
o	t	t	e	s	y	j	t	k	z	b	d	s
m	s	s	d	i	s	c	i	p	l	i	n	e

5 Rewrite the sentences in the passive. Use *by* + agent only where necessary.

1 Someone taught me to type when I was very young.
   I was taught to type when I was very young.

2 A nurse has just given us a talk on smoking.

3 Is someone going to announce the date of the next concert soon?

4 The headteacher is telling the students the result of their exams.

5 They never let students go into the staffroom.

6 The government paid the headteacher thousands of dollars.

7 Did someone give you that bicycle for your birthday?

8 A policeman made me cross the road on a proper crossing.

6 Rewrite these sentences correctly.

1 This work must to be rewritten!
   This work must be rewritten!

2 Your desk needs to be fixing.

3 We've had installed new computers in our school library.

4 Last week, I got my brother do my homework for me!

5 Has anything been doing to solve your problem yet?

6 In my opinion, holidays they should definitely be longer!

7 My hair needs to cut.

8 I wasn't let to go to the club last weekend.

7 Complete the blog with one word in each space.

View previous comments   Cancel Share Post

If I 1) _____were_____ asked what 2) _____ be done to improve my school, I'd have a lot of suggestions. The biggest thing that 3) _____ changing is the timetable. We 4) _____ taught a huge variety of subjects, but I want to study subjects that I find exciting. I think the timetable ought to 5) _____ planned much more around individuals and their interests. Another thing that needs 6) _____ be changed is the rule about uniforms. At my sister's school they are 7) _____ to wear what they like, but at my school we are 8) _____ to wear this awful uniform, even in senior classes. It's ridiculous!

Write a comment   Support

8 Rewrite the sentences using the words in capitals. Use between two and five words, including the word given.

1 Mum's getting someone to paint her nails for her.
   PAINTED
   Mum's *getting/having her nails painted* .

2 Someone ought to fix that broken window.
   NEEDS
   That window _____ .

3 That work was supposed to be done by now.
   SHOULD
   That work _____ by now.

4 Nobody let us miss lessons.
   WERE
   We _____ lessons.

5 They're going to offer our teacher promotion.
   IS
   Our teacher _____ promotion.

6 I got someone to update my laptop.
   HAD
   I _____ .

7 They really must change the timetable.
   BE
   The timetable really _____ .

8 Dad made me wash the dishes last night.
   GOT
   Dad _____ last night.

08 Technology rules!

READING

1 **Read the article and complete the words in the sentences so that they summarise it correctly.**

1 Being sent to your bedroom used to be a pu _nishment_ , but now it is a pleasure.

2 Parents worry that their children may become a_____ to gaming.

3 They worry that teens will confuse the computer-generated world with r_____ .

4 People wonder whether texting has replaced face-to-face co_____ with friends.

5 Some teenagers who have put personal stuff on the Internet have been b_____ by cruel people.

6 You can ac_____ information and ideas for essays on the Internet.

7 Multi_____ can be very distracting so it's not a good idea to use a lot of social devices while trying to do homework.

8 It's hard to con_____ on doing your homework if your phone is always bleeping with messages from your friends.

2 **Read the article again. Choose which sentence (a-g) fits each space (1-6) in the text. You do not need one of the sentences.**

a In other words, texting doesn't replace hanging out with friends in real life – it's just an extra way of catching up with them.

b Don't get me wrong – I love my digital world.

c It's what happens if you misinterpret what someone says online.

d They worry that the kind of casual language we use for texting, 'text speak', will affect our other communicative skills.

e Of course parents sometimes disapprove of the time we spend in the digital world.

f The fact that you can post your new achievements online for all the world to see provides great motivation!

g If your personal details or intimate conversations fall into the wrong hands it can lead to a lot of trouble.

3 **Choose the correct answer, A, B, C or D.**

1 According to the writer, parents worry that too much use of technology is ...
   A bad for mental and physical development.
   B a harmful distraction from real life.
   C likely to prevent us from making friends.
   D an addiction that damages the brain.

2 The writer says research results have shown that interest in face-to-face contact ...
   A increases as a result of frequent texting.
   B increases among older teens.
   C is not related to interest in texting.
   D is not lower among teens who text frequently.

3 The writer says that texting ...
   A provides good writing practice.
   B isn't very useful in the adult world.
   C doesn't change attitudes to formal writing.
   D provides us with information and ideas.

4 According to the article, the great benefit of the online world is ...
   A the very wide range of opportunities that it offers.
   B its usefulness for people with special interests.
   C the way it can improve writing skills.
   D the added interest it gives to lessons.

5 The writer admits that over-use of digital media can ...
   A make your homework take longer.
   B become addictive for a few people.
   C have a damaging effect on your mind.
   D make sleeping difficult unless you control it.

TEENAGERS AND THE DIGITAL WORLD

In the old days parents used to punish teenagers by sending them to their bedrooms but what was once a punishment has now become a pleasure. Why? Because teens are no longer isolated in their rooms. If you have a tablet or phone or similar device (and who hasn't these days!) you can really enjoy private time by texting friends and networking.

1) _e_ They worry that by using technology too much we are over-wiring our brains! They think if we spend too much time texting we'll forget how to socialise face to face, or that we'll get addicted to gaming, or that we'll confuse the computer-generated world with reality. But teenagers are not stupid. The idea that we are going to turn into zombies, bodies without minds who can't think for ourselves or connect with other people in real life, is ridiculous.

Research has shown that the teenagers who text their friends most often have most face-to-face contact with friends too. 2)_____ And when teenagers get to the age of eighteen or nineteen and are given more freedom to stay out, research shows they don't text as much.

Working out how to behave online takes a bit of practice, of course, and we all make mistakes in the beginning. Privacy can be a problem and you need to be careful who you share information with. 3)_____ There are plenty of stories of kids who've been teased or bullied over an unfortunate photo they've posted online or a careless remark that nobody but a friend was meant to see.

Another criticism that parents – and teachers – sometimes make is that texting is making teenagers write incorrectly. 4)_____ Again, research proves them wrong. The truth is, teenagers know it's important to write correctly if you want to be taken seriously in the adult world – and that we need to practise it now. Using text language won't prevent us learning to write formally. And with the Internet we can access information and ideas to use in essays and thus improve our writing.

Access to the online world helps us to be more creative as well. We can publish blogs that can be seen, not just by friends, but, by people all over the world. Or we can contribute articles to websites devoted to our special interests, like wildlife or movies. Teachers have begun to realise how this digital world can help in the classroom too. The amazing software on offer on the Internet can be used to awaken your interest in things you've never tried before, like art or composing music. 5)_____

Of course spending too much time online is bad, and multitasking can be distracting. If you keep jumping from chatrooms to YouTube or to online games while doing your homework, the results may not be good! You may also lose your ability to concentrate for long periods of time, if you're not careful! Personally, I find switching off all my electronic devices for an hour before bedtime is quite useful 6)_____ I'm as addicted as anyone to my tablet and my mobile. I just find that having one hour in the day to read or just think my own thoughts without interruption is actually quite cool.

Try it yourself – you may just find you like it too!

VOCABULARY
Technology

1 Label the items in the pictures.

computer   games console
keyboard   mouse   ~~screen~~

1   screen   2

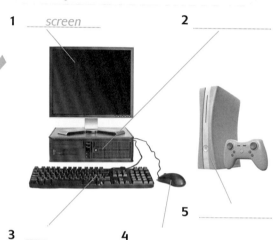

3 _____   4 _____

5 _____

2 Complete the sentences with these words in the correct form.

access   boast   ~~edit~~   flirt   gossip
misinterpret   swap   tease

1   I've typed my story so now I need to _edit_ it and send off for the competition.
2   Can I _____ pens with you for a minute? I can write much better with that one.
3   If you're going to _____ about me, you could at least get your facts right!
4   Ben is always _____ about how clever he is. He makes me sick!
5   Jessica _____ what I said and now she won't speak to me at all.
6   My friends are always _____ me because I have really thin legs.
7   Go to an Internet café and you can _____ the Internet and have a coffee, too!
8   My brother and my best friend are so keen on each other it's embarrassing – they're always _____ in the corridor.

3 Choose the correct answer, A, B, C or D.

1   My friends and I joined an online _____ room to discuss our problem.
    A chat   **B** gossip   **C** talk   **D** discuss
2   There weren't enough books so we had to _____ .
    A buy   **B** lend   **C** share   **D** borrow
3   I've just _____ a blog on the Internet.
    A sent   **B** messaged   **C** made   **D** posted
4   When Peter looks at Facebook, he'll see that I've left a 'Happy Birthday' message on his _____ .
    A clip   **B** wall   **C** modem   **D** screen
5   Look on YouTube and you'll see a _____ of Ben and I at last night's gig.
    A hit   **B** film   **C** clip   **D** snap
6   Please don't order me about in class. I'm not your _____ !
    A slave   **B** waiter   **C** prey   **D** victim
7   Do you know who first _____ the Internet?
    A discovered   **B** found   **C** manufactured   **D** invented
8   Don't worry if you can't print out your essay – we'll _____ the problem somehow!
    A get about   **B** get off   **C** get round   **D** get into

4 Find ten words on the topic of technology. The words go across, down or diagonally. The first letter of each word is highlighted.

v	l	m	e	f	r	o	u	t	e	r	e	y	v	c
y	p	v	e	k	b	g	t	q	l	f	g	l	t	a
j	s	y	m	o	m	l	k	b	l	b	e	c	w	w
h	d	i	a	o	y	p	o	c	s	c	r	e	e	n
c	f	p	t	z	u	o	s	r	a	x	r	i	z	n
g	u	n	v	e	p	s	o	n	l	i	n	e	q	z
h	a	n	a	d	u	a	e	c	l	o	x	l	n	n
g	k	d	g	i	a	s	t	r	o	n	o	m	y	o
c	e	c	g	r	d	i	h	r	d	n	t	l	y	r
u	y	i	i	e	b	i	v	p	i	g	s	s	k	s
g	b	h	x	c	t	p	q	t	g	e	u	o	y	v
s	o	v	x	t	s	j	j	i	x	a	p	l	b
a	a	z	o	o	h	j	m	e	t	y	o	z	v	e
w	r	g	b	r	o	a	d	b	a	n	d	z	f	c
o	d	e	u	a	k	x	r	y	l	b	l	g	n	o

GRAMMAR
Reported speech

1 Complete the reported questions by putting the words in the correct order.

1 The headteacher wanted to know / we / done / what / had / .
The headteacher wanted to know what we had done.

2 The shop assistant asked / us / help / could / if / he / .

3 My dad wanted to know / where / I / been / had / .

4 My friend wondered / free / go / was / if / to / out / I / .

5 Marie asked / whether / was / gig / going / Jamie / the / to / .

6 We wanted to know / working / why / not / was / computer / the / .

7 I asked / knew / singer / of / the / Tracy / she / name / the / if / .

8 John asked / seen / clip / I / if / his / YouTube / had / on / .

2 Finish putting the direct speech quotes into reported speech.

1 Someone wrote a nice comment on Linda's wall.
I was told that *someone had written a nice comment on Linda's wall* .

2 I'm starting a new school next term.
The boy next door said ___ .

3 What time are you going out?
Dad wanted to know ___ .

4 Did you remember to buy your aunt a birthday card?
Mum wanted to know ___ .

5 We're going to book a holiday in France, so you can practise your French.
My parents announced that ___ .

6 Have you found the money you lost?
My friend wondered ___ .

7 Adam's just gone to get his book.
I told the teacher ___ .

8 I dropped Adele's ring and now we can't find it.
I explained to Peter that ___ .

3 Read this conversation between George and his grandad. Then put it into reported speech, making all necessary changes.

Grandad: 1) Can you help with something, George?
George: 2) What's the problem, Grandad?
Grandad: 3) I'm having trouble with my laptop. I can't get my emails.
George: 4) Are you sure you've got an Internet connection?
Grandad: 5) I'm not sure, but it was working OK yesterday.
George: 6) I'll just check. There may be a problem with our telephone line.
Grandad: 7) Oh, does that affect the Internet?
George: 8) Yes it does, Grandad! But don't worry, I'll get your laptop working again soon.

1 *Grandad asked me if I could help him with something.*
2 ___
3 ___
4 ___
5 ___
6 ___
7 ___
8 ___

4 Complete the text with one word in each space.

Hacking – Is it a Crime?

I was doing a project on hacking, so I asked the teacher 1) *if/whether* he knew the name of the most famous hacker in the world. He 2) ___ me it was a man called Kevin Mitnik. Mitnik spent five years in jail for breaking into the computer systems of some major companies. But he claimed 3) ___ wasn't guilty of many of these crimes. He complained that the media 4) ___ misrepresented him. He admitted that he 5) ___ a hacker, but said that, for him, hacking was not something bad. When journalists asked him 6) ___ he believed that, he told 7) ___ that hacking used to be respected as a skill. He 8) ___ he'd never tried to steal credit card information or to rob anyone. But is hacking really a respectable activity? What do *you* think ?

USE OF ENGLISH
Vocabulary: abstract nouns

1 Complete the table.

	Verb	Noun	Adjective
1	civilise	civilisation	civilised
2	involve		xxxxxx
3	xxxxxx	democracy	
4	pollute		
5	achieve		achievable
6	observe		observable
7	encourage		encouraging

2 Complete the sentences with the correct form of the word in capitals.

1 Getting a first class Honours degree would be a great .... ACHIEVE
2 Sarah made a really clever .... in class today. OBSERVE
3 I had no .... in arranging the tennis competition at all, so don't blame me! INVOLVE
4 We've been studying the Mayan .... in our history classes. CIVILISE
5 Our teachers are great because they give us so much .... ENCOURAGE
6 Do you know how many countries in the world have .... governments? DEMOCRACY

3 Use the clues to complete the crossword.

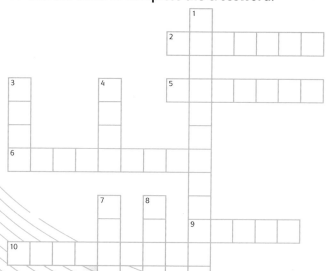

Across

2 The organs in your body that clean your blood.
5 If you have a .... camera, you can review and delete your photos.
6 The noun you can form from *know*.
9 To *get* .... *something* is a phrasal verb which means *to overcome a problem*.
10 The adjective you can form from *obstinacy*.

Down

1 To understand something wrongly
3 To .... *something up* is a phrasal verb which means *to support or confirm something*.
4 The place where friends write messages to you on Facebook.
7 To behave towards someone in a way that shows you may be attracted to them
8 To give something to someone in exchange for something else

4 Complete the article with the correct form of the words in capitals.

The Greatest Invention?

Among the great 1) _achievements_ of all time, which would you put top? Past 2) .... might have chosen sending a man into space. But for me, the greatest achievement of all time is the invention of the Internet. Now we can access information and increase our general 3) .... with one click of a key. Now we can meet friends at any time of day on 4) .... networking sites, or make video clips with friends and upload them for all the world to see. Networking sites can have disadvantages, though. Some parents feel their child's 5) .... is being invaded, or that the wrong people may be able to view their personal details. But in spite of these 6) .... , sites like Facebook are 7) .... popular. A word of warning though! Teachers and future employers may see what you put on the net. Post photos of yourself behaving badly and you'll leave them with a poor 8) .... of your character!

ACHIEVE

CIVILISE

KNOW

SOCIETY

PRIVATE

OBJECT
EXTREME

IMPRESS

USE OF ENGLISH
Grammar focus: reporting verbs

1 Complete the sentences with these verbs in their correct form. Use each verb once only.

> admit   invite   order   persuade   remind
> suggest   thank   ~~warn~~

1 My friends __*warned*__ me that making friends with the class bully was a big mistake.
2 Thank goodness you _____ me to take my phone with me; I couldn't have got help without it.
3 Wendy _____ meeting in the Internet café. Is that OK with you?
4 I didn't want to go to the pool, but in the end my little brother _____ me to take him there.
5 The policeman _____ the gang members to empty their pockets.
6 Darren _____ to me that he had dropped the MP3 player and broken it.
7 Has Bob _____ you to go to the cinema with him? He's shy about asking you!
8 We _____ our neighbours for looking after the cat and gave them a gift.

2 Complete the sentences in reported speech.

1 I'm sorry I hurt your feelings.
  Kylie apologised __*for hurting my feelings*__.
2 I'm so tired!
  Robert complained _____.
3 I wish I hadn't bought this make of camera.
  She regretted _____.
4 Go on! Make a clip for YouTube, Paul!
  I encouraged Paul _____.
5 Let's go out.
  My friend suggested _____.
6 Would you like to come to my party, James?
  I invited _____.
7 Sit down and be quiet!
  The teacher ordered me _____.
8 It's true – I did borrow your phone without asking you.
  Paul admitted _____.

3 Identify the six sentences which contain one unnecessary word and correct them.

1 The company is believed to have it brought out a new version of their software.
2 The engineer he is thought to have repaired the fault.
3 The gang are not believed to have been stolen all the computers.
4 Hackers are said to have discovered some secret information.
5 It is said that technology will it have changed the world beyond recognition in 100 years' time.
6 Tablet computers are reported to be now being in use in most classrooms in this area.
7 It is claimed that the new make of tablet computer has some major faults.
8 The new brand of smartphone is thought to have been outsold all other brands.

4 Complete the second sentence so that it means the same as the first.

1 People say that robots may take over the world one day.
  SAID
  It __*is said that*__ robots may take over the world one day.
2 They believe that hackers have got past their computer security system.
  BELIEVED
  Hackers _____ past the police security system.
3 They report a new social network site is gaining popularity.
  REPORTED
  A new social network site _____ popularity.
4 People say we are too dependent on technology.
  ARE
  We _____ too dependent on technology.
5 They claim that the new software is the best on the market.
  TO
  The new software _____ the best on the market.
6 They say that a child created the latest best-selling phone app.
  IS
  A child _____ the latest best-selling phone app.
7 It is believed that the fire started due to a fault in a computer.
  HAVE
  The fire _____ due to a fault in a computer.

LISTENING

1 🔊 **8.1 Listen to eight conversations or talks. Match each one (1–8) with a topic (a–h).**

1	Conversation		a	a speaker's mother
2	Conversation		b	a TV programme
3	Conversation		c	shopping
4	Talk		d	tablet computer
5	Conversation		e	Internet problems
6	Talk		f	reading preferences
7	Conversation		g	social networking
8	Talk		h	a speaker's brother

2 🔊 **8.2 Listen again and choose the correct answer, A, B or C.**

1 You hear two people talking about tablets. What problem has the girl got with hers?
   - **A** She can't remove unwanted apps from it.
   - **B** She can't download software on it.
   - **C** The Internet keeps disconnecting.

2 You hear two people talking about reading preferences. What does the girl say about e-books?
   - **A** She prefers them to print books.
   - **B** She finds them easy to read.
   - **C** She thinks they're too expensive.

3 You hear a girl complaining about her mother. What has her mother done?
   - **A** invaded her private space
   - **B** deleted messages from her smartphone
   - **C** read messages from her boyfriend

4 You hear some information about a TV programme. What does the speaker say about it?
   - **A** Famous inventors will take part in it.
   - **B** It will feature a former rock star.
   - **C** It will include a scene from a novel.

5 You hear a teenager talking about his brother. What does he say about him?
   - **A** He's been told to give up playing computer games.
   - **B** His computer addiction is making him ill.
   - **C** He regularly loses his temper with the computer.

6 You hear someone talking about social networking. What do they say about cyber bullies?
   - **A** If you threaten to tell an adult, bullies usually stop.
   - **B** Don't think you can cope with cyber bullies alone.
   - **C** Cyber bullies are usually alone.

7 You will hear two people talking about shopping. What is the boy's problem?
   - **A** He can't resist the temptation to window shop.
   - **B** He needs a Saturday job to pay for his debts.
   - **C** He finds it too easy to spend money.

8 You hear a voicemail message to a computer company. Why is the person calling?
   - **A** to ask for assistance
   - **B** to discuss his computer
   - **C** to purchase equipment

SPEAKING SKILLS

1 Write a question tag for each sentence.

1 We all like texting, _____*don't we*_____ ?
2 It can be dangerous to shop online, _____ ?
3 We shouldn't be scared of cyber bullies, _____ ?
4 You've bought a lot of songs on iTunes this week, _____ ?
5 You don't agree with me, _____ ?
6 Let's move on to the next photo, _____ ?

2 Put the words in the correct order.

1 An e-reader / read books on. / you / to / use / is something
   An e-reader is something you use to read books on.

2 to / can / use / You / this device / music outdoors. / hear

3 print / it's / when / necessary / something. / to / You use this

4 something / is / scanning / texts. / This / you need / for

5 answer / to / You / this / texts. / need / someone's

6 what / is / can't / I / remember / called. / this /

3 Complete the conversations with one word or a contraction in each space.

1 A Can you remember the word ___for___ this? It's something you _____ to copy pages from a book?

B I think it's called a photo-copier _____ it?

2 A What do you _____ this? You need it _____ changing channels on the TV.

B Well, I should know that, _____ I? But I'm afraid I've no idea!

3 A You can _____ this device _____ connect your smartphone to your car radio. What's it _____?

B Oh, we saw one in the shop yesterday, _____ we? Let me think.

4 A This is _____ you use for moving the cursor on the computer. What's the word in English?

B I don't know. I'll look in the dictionary, _____ I?

5 A What are the _____ you use to listen to your iPod quietly on the bus?

B You mean headphones, _____ you?

6 A What do you call the thing you type _____ , when _____ a computer?

B We learned that word in the lesson today, _____ we? Oh, what _____ it?

WRITING

1 Write these linking words or phrases next to those with a similar meaning.

> furthermore   in conclusion   in the first place
> nevertheless   since   whereas

1 although _____
2 moreover _____
3 because _____
4 to start with _____
5 finally _____
6 in spite of that _____

2 Read the task below. Complete a plan for the article by choosing the correct answers.

> Write an article for our teen magazine in 140–190 words, describing the two items of technology that the modern teenager values the most and why. We will publish the best article next month.

1 What two items of technology do teenagers most value?

> mobile phone   laptop   personal contact

_____ and _____

2 Why do they value them?

> for keeping in contact   easy to please
> multi-use

_____ and _____

3 Title of article:

> Teen technology   Technology in the future
> Technology and communication

4 Plan for the article: 1st, 2nd, 3rd

> Implications for the future
> The two items that teens value most
> Reasons for each one

1st _____
2nd _____
3rd _____

3 Read the task again and write your own answer.

Revision Unit 8

1 Choose the correct word, A, B or C.

1 I know you came top in the test. There's no need to ....
   A gossip   **(B)** boast   C tease

2 You saw what happened, so will you .... my story?
   A put up   B stand up   C back up

3 Chris and I always .... CDs with each other after we've finished with them.
   A swap   B sort   C share

4 Did you know that a man called Douglas Engelbart .... the computer mouse?
   A discovered   B did   C invented

5 Pamela's dad is always buying the latest .... , like new smartphones and tablet computers.
   A appliances   B gadgets   C machines

6 At the weekend, I'm going to .... with some of my best mates.
   A hang up   B hang together   C hang out

7 I need to .... this music from iTunes onto my MP3 player.
   A download   B edit   C access

8 My YouTube clip is really popular – it's getting lots of ....
   A prints   B hits   C punches

2 Complete the sentences with words from the box.

> ~~broadband~~   digital   mouse   online
> screen   site   user   viral

1 How much do you pay per month for _broadband_ and who's your provider?

2 Tanya's YouTube clip has gone .... ; she's had thousands of hits.

3 Which .... should I go on to get information for my coursework?

4 To go .... , you need to be connected to the Internet.

5 The battery has gone flat in my .... , so now I can't move the cursor or type anything.

6 My brother is a big .... of Facebook. He's on it all the time!

7 You'll need to clean the .... of that computer. It's so dusty you can't read a word on it.

8 The .... revolution is changing our world very quickly.

3 Form nouns from the words below.

1 social   →   _society_
2 independent   →   ....
3 private   →   ....
4 know   →   ....
5 involve   →   ....
6 imagine   →   ....
7 assess   →   ....
8 evident   →   ....

4 Complete the words in the sentences.

1 The d _i g i t a_ l revolution has brought us mobile phones and tablets.

2 Teenagers are big users of social n .... w .... sites.

3 We must change our bro .... provider; this one is too expensive.

4 We made the bully c .... e .... to the cruel things he'd done.

5 How many letters are there on a computer k .... y .... d. Do you know?

6 I felt really p .... ck .... the first time I took an IT exam.

7 You should be careful what you write in an email in case people mis .... t .... it.

8 I don't want to be a s .... e to technology.

5 Identify the six sentences which contain one unnecessary word and correct them.

1 Freya wanted to know where ~~did~~ I got my smartphone from.

2 Mum told to my sister to stop using Facebook.

3 Toby wanted to know whether Clare she was coming to the party.

4 A friend asked me if I knew the French teacher's address.

5 My classmates insisted on they were right.

6 The technician suggested I turning the computer off and then on again.

7 Dad reminded me to look up the information.

8 The teacher explained us that he had been ill the previous day.

6 Choose the correct answer, A, B or C.

1 I asked my friend how long _____ .
- **(A)** she had been waiting
- **B** had she been waiting
- **C** had been she waiting

2 The policeman ordered Gloria _____ .
- **A** going to the police station
- **B** go to the police station
- **C** to go to the police station

3 Tom suggested _____ our own video clip.
- **A** making
- **B** us to make
- **C** us making

4 My sister apologised _____ at me.
- **A** for shouting
- **B** to shout
- **C** that she shouted

5 We encouraged Sue _____ her old phone.
- **A** into selling
- **B** to sell
- **C** that she sell

6 Vandals _____ broken into the computer room.
- **A** they said to have
- **B** they are said to have
- **C** are said to have

7 It _____ computer chips will become much smaller in the future.
- **A** is believed that
- **B** believed that
- **C** is believing that

8 A scientist is reported _____ a car that drives itself.
- **A** he has invented
- **B** to have invented
- **C** having invented

7 Complete the sentences with one word in each space.

Have you ever used your parents' credit card to buy 1) _something_ online? If you have, I'm sure your parents warned you 2) _____ take great care – and they were right to do so! Thieves 3) _____ believed to be making thousands of dollars from online fraud. My family were victims of this kind of fraud last month. My parents are very nervous of online shopping, but I persuaded 4) _____ to let me buy a pair of jeans from a new website. My friend advised me 5) _____ to use the site because it might not be safe, but I took no notice. A few days later, my mum got a call from the credit card company. They told her that $4,000 6) _____ been taken from our card in one go by fraudsters! Of course, I apologised to my parents 7) _____ being so stupid, but they were really angry. I really regret 8) _____ so careless – and I won't do any online shopping again for a long time!

8 Complete the second sentence so that it means the same as the first.

1 'I'll buy your old laptop, Jenny.'
OFFERED
Harry _offered to buy_ Jenny's old laptop.

2 'Shall we text the rest of the group?' Dan said.
SUGGESTED
Dan _____ the rest of the group.

3 They say that YouTube gets thousands of hits a day.
SAID
YouTube _____ thousands of hits a day.

4 'Did Berners Lee invent the Internet?'
WHETHER
My friend wanted to know _____ the Internet.

5 'We're sorry we didn't phone you yesterday, Amy.'
APOLOGISED
Amy's friends _____ .

6 They think children are coping well with the digital world.
THOUGHT
Children _____ well with the digital world.

7 'Turn off the television immediately,' my dad said.
ORDERED
My dad _____ the television.

8 It was impossible to stop Craig from playing on the computer.
INSISTED
Craig _____ on the computer.

READING

1 Read the extract from a story and choose the correct answer, A, B or C.

1 Clare's brother was _____ her behaviour.
- **(A)** used to
- **B** angry about
- **C** upset by

2 Clare _____ the letter she had received from her school.
- **A** hid
- **B** replied to
- **C** threw away

3 Some of Clare's friends had _____ a building.
- **A** broken into
- **B** damaged
- **C** destroyed

4 The neighbours had _____ about Clare recently.
- **A** complained
- **B** been positive
- **C** changed their opinion

5 Clare was no longer allowed to _____ .
- **A** leave the house
- **B** leave her room
- **C** talk to anyone

6 She knew that her chosen escape route was

_____ .
- **A** reasonably safe
- **B** easy to use
- **C** dangerous

2 Read the story again and choose the correct answer, A, B, C or D.

1 From Clare's opening comments, it seems that her brother
- **A** often behaved worse than Clare.
- **B** had thrown a glass at Clare's mother.
- **C** always did what Clare told him.
- **D** tried to sympathise with Clare.

2 The word *truanted* in line 8 means
- **A** missed school.
- **B** misbehaved at school.
- **C** been late for school.
- **D** had detention at school.

3 Clare belonged to a gang that
- **A** didn't expect to be understood.
- **B** had behaved liked vandals.
- **C** liked to set the fashion.
- **D** had been blamed unfairly.

4 The writer states that Clare's neighbours have
- **A** complained to her mother about her.
- **B** changed their opinion of her.
- **C** become very fond of her.
- **D** started complimenting her.

5 When Mrs Clark finally decided take action with her daughter,
- **A** she frightened her daughter.
- **B** she wasn't scared to do it.
- **C** she was too nervous to carry it out.
- **D** she had some worries about it.

6 The word *it* in *Would it hold her weight?* in line 39 refers to
- **A** the drainpipe.
- **B** the plan.
- **C** the water.
- **D** the roof.

Chapter 2

Broken lives

'You haven't got a clue how I'm feeling so don't pretend you do!' Clare yelled at her brother as she stormed out of the kitchen, slamming the door so hard the house seemed to shake.

'Here we go again,' she heard him sigh. She could just imagine him, obediently sweeping up the broken glass from the floor and comforting their mother.

5   'I might have known whose side you'd be on!' she yelled as she raced up the stairs.

Lying on her bed, she read through the letter that had caused the latest row. 'Clare's behaviour has been outrageous. She constantly defies the staff, completely neglecting to do her homework or handing it in late. Worse still, she has truanted on a number of occasions, thus missing important exam revision. Unless we see a significant improvement in her behaviour, we will have to exclude
10 her permanently.'

Clare screwed the letter into a tight ball and hurled it out of the window in fury. 'Exclude me then! Who cares?' she yelled, burying her face in the pillow.

Some time later, when her thoughts had calmed a little, she sat up. She was desperate to call Harry, the latest of her friends to be labelled 'unsuitable' by her dear parents. So what if his clothes
15 were weird? 'He's a trendsetter. He leads and everyone follows,' she had told her mum. But it was pointless. Her mum would never understand. He was the leader of the gang she hung out with so her parents automatically assumed he was bad news. Alright, the group didn't always behave like angels. The graffiti on the Town Hall hadn't got there by magic. 'What do they expect? There's nothing to do in this stupid village!' she'd complained. But her words had fallen on deaf ears, as usual.

20 Downstairs, her mum was sitting at the kitchen table, head in hands. 'Where did we go wrong,' she sighed to herself. It seemed like only yesterday that her daughter had been a model child. 'What a lovely daughter you've got!' neighbours were always telling her. Not anymore though. These days Clare was like an alien from another planet – a rebel who over recent weeks had managed to break all the rules. When told to help with chores or do homework, she'd just roll her eyes or answer back.
25 She'd stay out late and then refuse to say where she'd been. Now she was even beginning to skip school. What on earth had got into her?

'It's no good, we have to get serious,' Clare's mum told her dad on his return from work. 'I vote we ground her,' she continued.

'I'd go along with that!' her dad replied. 'Take her key off her so she can't slip out undetected.
30 But we should take her mobile phone and computer off her as well. That way she can't contact Harry and get into mischief.'

It had seemed like a good plan at the time; less so the next day when the time came to actually do it. She didn't like to admit it but Mrs Clark was a little scared of her daughter.

Clare was speechless when she was told her punishment. Being restricted to the house was bad
35 enough, but texting and networking with friends was her whole life. The way her parents were treating her was way over the top – it was so unfair! But what could she do? Glancing out of the window, she saw the rickety drainpipe that carried water from the roof to the ground. Climb down, run to Harry's house and they could run away together. Yes, good plan! But it didn't look very firm. Would it hold her weight? There was only one way to find out. Taking a deep breath, she swung her
40 legs over the windowsill and round the swaying drainpipe.

'Here we go,' she whispered uncertainly to herself as she started her shaky descent.

20

VOCABULARY
Personality and behaviour

1 Decide if the adjectives describe good or bad qualities and put them in the correct list.

> cruel   disrespectful   easy-going
> fussy   generous   polite   rebellious
> stubborn   tolerant   unselfish
> ~~well-behaved~~

Good qualities
well-behaved

....

....

....

....

....

Bad qualities

....

....

....

....

....

2 Complete the sentences with the correct form of the word in capitals.

1 Tom's ___rebellion___ against the school rules led to him being expelled.
REBEL

2 My sister got a prize for good ....
BEHAVE

3 Our uncle died last year so my aunt is now ....
WIDOW

4 Paul is really kind and ....
HELP

5 Dad's pleased because my school report says there's been a great .... in my attitude to school!
IMPROVE

6 Laura got on much better in class after the .... of the new teacher.
ARRIVE

7 I can't believe you were so .... to your gran. You were really rude!
RESPECT

8 My little brother is terribly .... and is always getting told off.
OBEDIENT

3 Complete the sentences with these words.

> giggle   hit   nightmare   open   rude   ~~sight~~

1 When my mum met my dad, it was love at first ___sight___!

2 My penfriend came to stay last week and we didn't get on; in fact, she was a total .... !

3 Fran gets on well with her teacher, so perhaps she'll .... up to him about the problem.

4 Mum .... the roof when she saw my tattoo!

5 I got a .... awakening when I came bottom of the class this year!

6 My friend and I wore awful, coloured wigs to the party just for a ....

4 Choose the correct word, A, B or C.

1 I'm sorry, but I don't want to .... with you about this any more.
  A dispute   **(B)** argue   **C** dialogue

2 I really .... having to wash the dishes every evening.
  A object   **B** resent   **C** refuse

3 If Grace is rude to you, just try and .... it.
  A neglect   **B** reject   **C** ignore

4 I hate having .... with my family, but they never last long.
  A lines   **B** rows   **C** bans

5 My parents only give me pocket money if I help with the household ....
  A jobs   **B** works   **C** chores

6 Dad's .... me from going to the youth club for a month.
  A forbidden   **B** banned   **C** ordered

GRAMMAR
Modal verbs

1 Choose the correct answer, A, B or C.

1 Duncan _____ speak French really well.
A ought
B is able
C can

2 You _____ shout at me – I'm not doing anything wrong.
A needn't
B can't
C don't need

3 Why _____ argue with Peter? He's really upset now.
A did you ought to
B could you
C did you have to

4 You _____ try to buy alcohol if you're under the legal age to do so.
A mustn't
B couldn't
C don't need to

5 I'm sure Emma _____ be out alone so late at night – do her parents know where she is?
A can't
B shouldn't
C doesn't need

6 I'm really annoyed that I _____ to go to the music festival last weekend.
A wasn't let
B couldn't
C wasn't allowed

2 Complete the sentences with modal verbs in the positive or negative form. There may be more than one correct answer.

1 I know I ___*must*___ not use bad language so don't worry, I'll be careful.

2 Why did you _____ go to bed so early last night? What had you done wrong?

3 How _____ you speak to your mum like that? Apologise at once!

4 Hurray! It's a holiday tomorrow so I _____ to get up early.

5 I _____ text you yesterday because my dad has taken my phone off me!

6 If I were you, I _____ see a doctor about your cough.

3 Complete the text with one word in each space.

💬 View previous comments   Cancel Share Post

How to deal with bullies
There are lots of bullies around. You 1) ___*can*___ find them at school, and at work, too. Mike was our school bully. He was a big guy and he scared the younger kids so much they felt they 2) _____ to do everything he told them. They were never 3) _____ to disagree – they didn't dare, because they knew Mike 4) _____ make their lives very difficult if he wanted – by putting cruel remarks on Facebook, for example, or telling lies about them. So, why was Mike a bully? Well, like all bullies he had personal problems that he could 5) _____ – or would not – discuss. Because he had no confidence in himself, he felt he 6) _____ to make his victims feel insecure, too. Luckily, Mike's victims soon realised that they didn't have 7) _____ put up with his behaviour. Their friends had already advised them that they 8) _____ tell the headteacher. They did, and Mike soon found himself in the headteacher's office. There was no more bullying at our school for a very long time after that.

Write a comment   Support

4 Rewrite the sentences using the words in capitals. Use between two and five words, including the word given.

1 You don't have to come if you don't want to.
NEED
You ___*needn't/don't need to come*___ if you don't want to.

2 My advice is to talk to your parents about it.
OUGHT
I think you _____ to your parents about it.

3 Our parents didn't let us stay out late last night.
ALLOWED
We _____ out late last night.

4 We were obliged to help with the housework.
TO
We _____ with the housework.

5 I'm sorry I couldn't go on the trip with you.
ABLE
I'm sorry I _____ on the trip with you.

6 You can't go to that club if you're under eighteen.
GOT
You _____ eighteen to go to that club.

7 It's compulsory to obey the rules if you want to join our gang.
HAVE
You _____ the rules if you want to join our gang.

USE OF ENGLISH
Vocabulary: trouble

1 Choose the correct word.

1 We *felt/took* sorry for the new girl and let her join our gang.
2 My brother is so spoiled that he shouts and screams if he can't *get/go* his own way.
3 Maria stole my boyfriend, but I'll *get/make* my own back one day!
4 I've *done/made* friends with the boy next door.
5 The bully soon *backed/stood* down when the teacher came into the room.
6 Ryan got left *down/out* of the football team for the match on Friday and he's so disappointed.
7 I'm sorry if I upset you; please don't let us *fall/walk* out.
8 Pay no attention to George; he's just trying to *do/make* trouble.

2 Complete the sentences with these words.

arrest   burgle   charge   ~~interview~~
judge   mug   probation   victim

1 The police decided to take the man back to the police station and *interview* him.
2 Always lock your door when you go out in case somebody tries to break in and _____ your house.
3 Don't make it obvious you're carrying so much cash, or somebody might _____ you.
4 For one year after leaving jail, the woman had to report to her _____ officer every month.
5 If you drink and drive, the police may stop you, _____ you and take you to a police station.
6 The _____ sent the murderer to jail for life.
7 The police took the man to the police station, but they couldn't _____ him because they didn't have enough evidence.
8 The _____ of the robbery was shocked but not injured, thank goodness.

3 Complete the article with the best answer, A, B, C or D.

Subject: **My new house!**

My brother William had a 1) *rude* awakening last week. He'd recently 2) _____ friends with a gang of teenagers who my parents really didn't like. The gang were always 3) _____ trouble in our neighbourhood, especially when they 4) _____ out with other teenage gangs. Anyway, last week my brother thought a neighbour was making 5) _____ of his new haircut, so he started a fight. A police car arrived soon afterwards, and the officer said he was going to 6) _____ William. William was defiant at first, but he 7) _____ down when a police dog jumped out of the car! He then realised he was in big trouble and stared crying! Luckily for William, his victim was kind-hearted and felt 8) _____ for him. He asked the policeman to let William off with a warning. I don't think my brother will be hanging out with a gang again for a long time!

1 **A** rude   **B** sad   **C** rough   **D** large
2 **A** done   **B** been   **C** made   **D** formed
3 **A** doing   **B** making   **C** being   **D** getting
4 **A** fell   **B** went   **C** fought   **D** did
5 **A** laugh   **B** fun   **C** enjoyment **D** silly
6 **A** suspend **B** charge   **C** arrest   **D** exclude
7 **A** jumped **B** went   **C** stood   **D** backed
8 **A** sad   **B** pity   **C** unhappy   **D** sorry

4 Find ten words in the wordsearch on the topic of personality and behaviour. The words go across, down or diagonally. The first letter of each word is highlighted.

e	w	f	o	a	q	n	n	f	l	f	j	i	w	n
q	s	r	s	g	j	a	l	s	r	a	c	h	e	d
j	j	k	f	e	c	s	p	v	u	c	h	z	o	d
m	w	y	m	n	r	t	m	t	g	q	a	u	c	i
i	c	e	m	e	b	y	e	o	a	b	r	q	n	y
q	z	a	c	r	x	g	n	b	u	c	m	h	p	m
b	x	s	f	o	v	w	v	n	r	l	i	r	c	s
m	q	y	l	u	i	v	i	o	a	o	n	d	s	p
w	c	g	e	s	h	g	r	x	l	a	g	n	p	i
z	l	o	x	w	s	m	o	i	d	r	b	x	o	t
p	f	i	i	h	h	o	n	o	p	f	m	z	i	e
l	e	n	b	y	y	o	m	u	v	p	d	w	l	f
z	b	g	l	s	b	d	e	s	o	f	s	c	e	u
r	p	f	e	b	j	y	n	e	f	s	l	c	d	l
f	u	w	a	j	o	u	t	r	a	g	e	o	u	s

USE OF ENGLISH
Grammar: more modals

1 Choose the correct answer.

1 Oh, you *shouldn't have/needn't have* been so unkind to Paula! She was only trying to help.

2 Bob *didn't have to/couldn't have* do detention after all.

3 Conrad *mustn't have/shouldn't have* told a lie, but he did.

4 The gang *might have/must have* left that graffiti on the wall, but I'm not sure.

5 You *ought to have/needed to have* reported the theft to the police.

6 I *needn't have/could have to* texted an apology to Sarah, but I did it anyway.

7 I *could have/might have* killed Jane for posting my secret on Facebook!

8 We knew Sandra was getting the bus here so we *didn't need to get/needn't have got* the car out.

2 Choose the correct answer, A, B or C.

1 The burglars _____ broken into the house last night because the alarm was on.
   A needn't have
   B didn't need to
   C couldn't have

2 I _____ worried about starting at my new school because everybody is so friendly.
   A didn't need to
   B couldn't have
   C needn't have

3 You _____ left your keys in the cafeteria. Shall I go back and check?
   A could
   B need have
   C might have

4 You _____ to have left your room in such a mess, Freddie!
   A ought not
   B could not
   C should not

5 Luckily, I had money for a taxi so I _____ .
   A needn't have walked
   B couldn't have walked
   C didn't need to walk

6 You shouldn't have cycled on that busy road. You _____ killed!
   A could have been
   B ought to have been
   C might be

3 Identify the six sentences which contain a mistake and correct them.

1 Paul can have gone to the party, but I'm not sure.
   Paul could have gone to the party, but I'm not sure.

2 He couldn't be in the café last night. If he were, I'd have seen him.

3 I needn't paid so much for that jacket – I should have gone to another shop.

4 You should have told me you were feeling ill and I would have called a doctor.

5 I'm glad I needn't go to school yesterday – it was great spending time on the beach.

6 Gina isn't here yet – her bus might have broken down.

7 I may leave my phone on the bus so I'd better get back on and look.

8 Tom must have texted Linda, but I'm not sure.

4 Complete the sentences with one word only.

1 I think I *may/might* have hurt Maria's feelings.

2 You ought _____ have discussed the problem with your teacher.

3 It was so nasty of you to say that! You really _____ have apologised for your actions.

4 We didn't _____ to stay late after all because the exam was shorter than we thought.

5 Sally's plane _____ have landed already, but we're not certain.

6 I'm glad I _____ not need to sit next to Carlos today; he's such a bully.

LISTENING

1 🔊 **9.1 Listen to a discussion about romantic relationships. Tick (✓) the topics that are discussed.**

1 trust ✓
2 jealousy ......
3 respect ......
4 safety ......
5 break-ups ......
6 recovery ......

2 🔊 **9.2 Listen again and choose the correct answer, A, B, or C.**

1 According to Sarah, if you trust someone
   Ⓐ you know you can rely on them.
   B you may still get jealous of them.
   C you have something to build on.

2 Sarah says that having respect for someone involves
   A listening to their problems.
   B sharing their interests.
   C accepting their differences.

3 Sarah says that if you persuade an ex to meet up again
   A they may change their minds.
   B you may feel more unwanted.
   C it can help to clear the air.

4 Sarah advised anyone whose relationship ends to
   A return unwanted gifts.
   B avoid reminders of the past.
   C throw away valuable presents.

5 Sarah thinks that if you need a good cry you should
   A make sure you're at home.
   B go out with friends instead.
   C do it when someone else is there.

6 Sarah says it's important not to
   A doubt your actions.
   B think badly of yourself.
   C blame the other person.

7 Sarah advises people to make a list so that they can
   A see how wonderful they are.
   B show it to friends.
   C use it to find a new partner.

SPEAKING SKILLS

1 **Complete the words and phrases used to interrupt when someone else is speaking.**

1 Ex _cuse_ me!
2 Can I j_____ in here?
3 Sorry to b_____ in, but …
4 Before you g_____ on, I'd like to say …
5 Sorry to i_____ , but could I say that … ?

2 **Choose the correct words to complete what a student said about these photos.**

1) *Each/Both* these photos show events from history. The one at the top was taken at the breaking down of the – I don't know how you 2) *say/tell* it – the Berlin wall? And the other is when the ruler of Iraq was defeated. The Iraq picture is 3) *quite/quiet* recent – say a decade or so ago – 4) *whereas/meanwhile* the other event was in the 20th century. I 5) *am/do* think history is important. We need to learn from past mistakes if we're going to avoid fighting and wars in the future. That's an 6) *extreme/extremely* important reason to study history, 7) *isn't/wasn't* it?

WRITING

1 Read the task and the email from Julia to Kate. Then read the first part of Kate's email response. Underline the six linking words or phrases in the response.

> You have received an email from your English pen pal, Julia. Read this part of the email and then write an email response.

Kate,

I split up with my boyfriend a few weeks ago and I'm really depressed. My parents are always nagging me to forget about it and go out more – why can't they understand how bad I feel? I've been having a lot of arguments with them because they won't leave me alone. I don't want to be with anyone else. My life is such a mess. What should I do?

Hi Julia

I'm so sorry you're feeling depressed. Losing a friend is always a horrible experience so no wonder you're feeling bad at the moment. I know a bit about how you feel because it's happened to me as well, although it was some time ago.

It can be hard to talk about these things, I know. However, I'm sure you'll find your friends are really sympathetic. After all, most of us have our hearts broken at some time! Why not arrange to meet them somewhere quiet and then tell them everything that's happened. They're probably worrying how you are, anyway. Don't try to hide your real feelings – just let it all out!

2 Read the next paragraph of the email response from Kate to Julia. Write these words and phrases in the correct spaces (1–6).

> Good luck   it gets easier with time
> if I were you   ~~maybe you could~~
> remember to   try

Now for your relationship with your parents. If you haven't done this already, 1) _maybe you could_ catch a quiet moment with your mum, when you're not feeling too angry or stressed. 2) _____ explaining to her exactly how you feel, without getting out of control. 3) _____ speak calmly and quietly instead of shouting or getting worked up. Remember that your mum – and your dad – were teenagers once themselves. You just have to remind them how they felt all those years ago – without antagonising them, of course!

4) _____, I would let the people around you know how deeply hurt you feel and how depressed you are. I'm sure they will want to help you, Julia. As I said before, it's hard to cope with losing any kind of friend, but 5) _____ so don't be too sad. One day you'll meet someone you like just as much as your ex-boyfriend, you'll see!

6) _____ Julia, and let me know how you're getting on.

love Kate

3 Write your own answer to the task in 140–190 words, using an appropriate style.

Revision Unit 9

1 Choose the correct word.

1 Clive is really *flexible/generous* – he gives a lot of money away to charity.
2 Somebody who is really *cruel/stubborn* will hurt another person for no reason at all.
3 My brother is so *moody/fussy* that you never know if he's going to be happy or sad from one day to the next.
4 Emma's boyfriend is really *well-mannered/tolerant* – he always holds the door open for women to go first.
5 Using bad language is *unselfish/disrespectful*, especially in front of older people.
6 Teenagers may feel *rebellious/nasty* if they're made to follow too many rules.
7 Mr Lee won't mind if you're late for youth club. He's very *helpful/easy-going*.
8 My little brother is really *disobedient/spiteful* – he never does what my parents tell him to do!

2 Complete the words in the sentences.

1 It was really sp *i* _ *t* _ *e* _ f _ *u* _ l of you to write such cruel remarks about me on Facebook.
2 My gran was w _____ d _____ when my grandfather was killed in the war.
3 We had a big party to celebrate my sister and her boyfriend getting en _____ d. The wedding's next year.
4 Our neighbour only got d _____ c ____ d last year and he's marrying someone new in September!
5 My mum and dad s ____ p _____ d when I was four, so my mum brought me up by herself.
6 I don't just dislike the boy next door; I think he's completely ob _____ x _____ s.
7 I'm reading a book about a kid who was a _____ p _____ d by a family of wolves after the death of her parents.
8 One of my brothers accepts what my parents say but the other is a rebel and is always extremely d ____ f _____ t.

3 Choose the correct answer, A, B or C.

1 We only wrote Peter's name on Anne's desk for a _____.
   A smile   **B** giggle   C grin
2 My teacher hit the _____ when he saw the mess in the classroom.
   A top   B ceiling   C roof
3 Pamela had a _____ awakening when the exam she'd thought would be easy turned out to be so difficult.
   A shock   B cruel   C rude
4 Sheila is as hard as _____, so you'll never persuade her to feel sorry for you.
   A nails   B metal   C iron
5 Ben is a good listener and people often _____ up to him about their problems.
   A give   B open   C show
6 Babysitting my neighbour's kid was an absolute _____ because he just wouldn't go to sleep.
   A nightmare   B dream   C torture

4 Complete the text with one word in each space.

Subject: **If you want to be a criminal!**

If you want to be a criminal, you need 1) *to* have at least a little bit of intelligence. Without it, you 2) _____ try as hard as you like, but you'll end up in prison one day! Take Jason Finch, for example. He decided to rob a bank. He 3) _____ have succeeded, too, if he hadn't written a note for the bank clerk on the back of his own cheque book. When the police arrived they did not 4) _____ to look for fingerprints or clues; they just identified the robber from his cheques and arrested him! One thing you 5) _____ never do as a criminal is to fall asleep on the job. A criminal set out to burgle a house in the USA. He 6) _____ easily have got away with the jewellery but he decided he had 7) _____ lie down on the bed and close his eyes for a few minutes. That bed must 8) _____ been really comfortable because 9) _____ the house owner arrived, the criminal was still fast asleep!

5 Complete the words in the sentences.

1 When criminals come out of jail, a
p _r_ _o_ _b_ at _i_ _o_ n officer often helps them
improve their lives.

2 A criminal is less likely to b _____ g _____ e your
house if you have an alarm fitted.

3 It's not safe to leave your car in this street because
the local gang might v _____ d _____ s _____ it.

4 Crazy people sometimes st _____ k celebrities,
which means they follow them round everywhere
they go.

5 People often end up in jail because of their
criminal b _____ h ____ v _____ .

6 The vandals were too young for jail so they were
put in d _____ e _____ i _____ .

7 The j _____ g _____ told the jury to take as much
time as they wanted to reach a decision.

8 The attacker left his v _____ t _____ m lying in the
street, badly injured.

6 Rewrite the sentences using the words in
capitals. Use between two and five words,
including the word given.

1 It's compulsory to follow the rules.
OBEY
You _must/have(got) to_ obey the rules.

2 Their teachers didn't let them leave school early.
ALLOWED
They _____ school early.

3 My advice is to report the bully to the
headteacher.
SHOULD
I think _____ to the headteacher.

4 We were obliged to do chores to earn our
pocket money.
TO
We _____ chores to earn our
pocket money.

5 I worried about the problem but it
wasn't necessary.
NEED
I _____ worried about the problem.

6 It would have been a good idea to text
our parents.
SHOULD
We _____ our parents.

7 It's possible I left my keys in the door.
COULD
I _____ my keys in the door.

7 Identify the six sentences which contain a mistake
and correct them.

1 Nobody could prevent the accident yesterday. ✗
Nobody could have prevented the accident yesterday.

2 You should have gone home earlier last night.

3 My parents weren't let to smoke when they
were children.

4 Did you have got to apologise for what you said?

5 I didn't need tell Mike the secret because he
knew already.

6 You must to obey your parents, I'm afraid.

7 Clare may have rung while I was in the shower –
I'll check.

8 When I was younger, I wasn't let to stay up late.

8 Use the clues to solve the crossword.

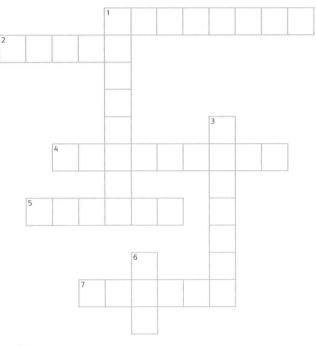

Across

1 A situation in which neither opponent is winning

2 The person who decides how criminals
are punished

4 An adjective which means hateful

5 If someone breaks the law, a policeman may
_____ them.

7 Jobs around the house

Down

1 Behaviour that shows you refuse to do what
someone tells you to do

3 To admit you are wrong

6 Another word for a quarrel or argument

READING

1 **Read the article and choose the correct answer, true or false.**

1 Pizarro's father was a poor man.
   True   <u>False</u>

2 Pizarro shared in the conquest of Mexico.
   True   False

3 The Incan people did not believe in gods.
   True   False

4 Atahualpa killed some of his relatives.
   True   False

5 The Spaniards behaved dishonestly.
   True   False

6 The Inca took gold from his own followers to give to the Spaniards.
   True   False

7 Atahualpa's soldiers betrayed him to the Spaniards.
   True   False

8 Pizarro was killed after returning home to Spain.
   True   False

9 Pizarro's death was a contrast to the life he led.
   True   False

2 **Read the article again. Which section (A–D), mentions:**

1 demanding money or treasure in exchange for something? _C_

2 trying to follow in someone's shoes? _____

3 treasures that were found at the Aztec empire after it was conquered? _____

4 a story about a final desperate action that might not be true? _____

5 being unaware of an immediate risk? _____

6 seeking thrills at a young age? _____

7 failing to value things of great worth? _____

8 believing someone has acted dishonestly? _____

9 being protected by supernatural power? _____

10 breaking a promise? _____

The ruins of the Incan city of Machu Picchu in present-day Peru.

Amazing battles

A

History is full of battles. Some decide the fate of kings, some of whole countries. One of the most amazing battles I know of took place five centuries ago when a leader with only 160 men and a few dozen horses defeated one of the largest civilisations in the world. The leader of the battle was a Spanish explorer called Francisco Pizarro. His father was a nobleman and a distinguished soldier, but he was not married to Pizarro's mother. With no hope of inheriting money or title, Pizarro joined the army while still in his teens, maybe because he admired his father or, as seems more likely, because it offered adventure. News soon reached him of the discovery and conquest of the Aztec empire in Mexico and of the precious metals that had been found there. Were there other kingdoms to be discovered in the Americas? Assembling a group of like-minded soldiers, he set sail to find out.

B

As he travelled through the land we now know as Peru, Pizarro heard tales of a hidden empire. He sailed back to Spain, obtained his King's permission to conquer the land, then returned to Peru with his soldiers. Once back, he found the country was at war with itself. The old ruler, had died and his sons had been battling for power. Atahualpa, the youngest son, had killed some siblings and captured another. Now he was the leader of the Incan people, which made him a deity. So busy was he with all this, he failed to see the danger posed by the invading Spaniards. It was, after all, a very small army the Spaniards had and he, the Inca ruler, had many thousands of soldiers – not with him, but scattered around his Empire. Besides, as an Incan leader he was now a god – and who would dare attack a deity? So relaxed did Atahualpa feel that he agreed to meet the invaders. It was, of course, a trap. Atahualpa was quickly captured and imprisoned.

C

Worse was to follow. While his followers were being murdered, Atahualpa bargained desperately for his life. Pizarro offered him a deal: pay a huge ransom of gold and silver, and he, Atahualpa, could go free. The Inca leader immediately commanded his followers to bring gold and silver treasures from all over the Empire – there were so many they filled a whole room. But beautiful as they were as objects, the Spaniards gave them no respect; they were all melted down into gold bars and sent to Spain. Atahualpa had now kept his side of the deal – not so the Spanish. They knew the Inca leader had thousands of loyal soldiers who might just overcome their fear of the foreigners and try to rescue him. Atahualpa was executed.

D

In one single battle Pizarro had conquered half of South America. He returned to the coast where he founded a port called Lima, and soon ships full of soldiers and clerks were arriving there, ready to govern the new empire. The Incan people tried to rebel in small groups but the Spanish were too strong. Meanwhile Pizarro was now rich and powerful and living in Lima. But wicked deeds do not always go unpunished. Over the years, Pizarro had made many enemies. Some of the men who'd fought with him suspected he'd taken more than his share of the treasure and land. Eventually he was attacked in his home and stabbed in the throat. As he died, he is rumoured to have drawn a cross in blood on the floor. It was a violent end for a man who had been no stranger to cruelty or violence all his life.

A statue of Francisco Pizarro in Trujillo, Spain.

VOCABULARY
History

1 Complete the sentences with the correct form of the word in capitals.

1 We saw the famous _____portrait_____ of King Henry hanging in the National Art Gallery.
PORTRAY

2 There has been great excitement over the _____ of Tutankhamen's tomb.
DISCOVER

3 The castle was destroyed during the great _____ in the 16th century.
REBEL

4 The tyrant was _____ and ordered all his prisoners to be killed.
MERCY

5 The new prince is a _____ of the ancient kings of Scotland.
DESCEND

6 Is there any real _____ that the ruler was murdered?
PROVE

7 I love studying the past and one day I'd like to be a famous _____ .
HISTORY

2 Choose the correct answer.

1 Adolf Hitler was an *unknown/infamous* figure who caused the deaths of millions of people.

2 Queen Elizabeth I is *unearthed/buried* in Westminster Abbey.

3 Royal families are often buried in beautifully decorated *tombs/trenches*.

4 There are no *records/portraits* of where the last Inca king is buried.

5 I love reading the Greek *rumours/myths*, like the story of Theseus and the Minotaur.

6 In *ancient/aged* times people believed their rulers – the pharaohs – were gods.

7 Archaeologists have discovered the *remains/rests* of a Roman temple.

8 The people who set up the United Nations wanted to prevent a third world *battle/war*.

3 Complete the sentences with these words.

> burial   contentious   curse   fever pitch
> ~~grave~~   mankind   mutilated   stumbled upon

1 They put the tyrant's body in an unmarked _____grave_____ where nobody would find it.

2 The ruler died while sailing round his country, so his _____ took place at sea.

3 Excitement rose to _____ as news of the amazing discovery spread through the country.

4 The king was murdered and parts of his _____ body were put on show round the city.

5 Nobody can agree about the causes of the war; the topic is extremely _____ .

6 Archaeologists _____ the body while they were searching for the remains of a palace.

7 There is a _____ on Tutankhamun's tomb which threatens bad things to anyone who enters it.

8 Throughout the history of _____ , there have been many battles and wars.

4 Find ten words on the topic of history. The words go across, down or diagonally. The first letter of each word is highlighted.

a	u	e	z	g	d	g	g	l	e	n	o	a	s	l
r	c	i	r	r	d	f	u	s	d	u	n	n	h	r
e	q	x	o	a	f	r	v	t	m	t	j	e	i	m
u	r	c	o	y	n	r	e	e	r	o	m	i	s	j
k	e	j	y	r	f	e	r	p	x	m	t	j	t	e
r	e	j	f	e	c	m	h	r	x	b	z	b	o	q
r	b	z	q	h	q	a	d	a	m	n	j	x	r	j
e	x	z	a	e	i	i	m	s	a	d	m	w	i	j
b	s	k	v	a	b	n	d	u	q	j	m	k	a	j
e	a	f	f	r	t	s	d	s	t	y	r	a	n	t
l	o	d	e	s	c	e	n	d	a	n	t	q	v	t
l	n	l	o	a	m	w	p	p	m	b	y	e	e	g
i	l	f	g	l	w	g	r	a	v	e	d	d	t	i
o	u	b	n	h	p	k	j	b	u	r	i	a	l	u
n	e	x	c	a	v	a	t	i	o	n	t	n	o	v

GRAMMAR
Relative clauses

1 **Choose the correct word.**

1 Is this one of the castles *that/what* you have already visited?

2 Richard is the king *who/whose* nephews were killed in the Tower.

3 Paul's the teacher *who/which* will be teaching us history next term.

4 A dinosaur was an animal *who/which* lived thousands of years ago.

5 She works in a museum *that/it* used to be part of a temple.

6 The town *where/that* I grew up has a long history.

7 Can you remember the date *which/when* the war started?

8 I've just seen the house *where/that* I was born.

2 **Complete the sentences by adding the information in brackets. You may need to change the order of the clauses.**

1 The Valley of the Kings is a place in Egypt. (The tombs of many Pharaohs were uncovered there.)
   The Valley of the Kings is a place in Egypt where the tombs of many pharaohs were found.

2 There is a temple in the city.
   (It holds amazing treasures.)

3 The queen's uncle was arrested and executed.
   (He put poison in the king's drink.)

4 Our country has plenty of castles.
   (They are all open to the public most weekdays.)

5 I've just read about a king.
   (His children joined in a rebellion against him.)

6 We took a photo of the palace.
   (The royal family still live in it.)

7 The armour can be seen in the museum.
   (The king fought in it.)

8 The crown is in the museum.
   (I visited it yesterday.)

3 **Complete the spaces with appropriate relative or participle clauses using the words in brackets.**

1 We visited the tomb, then wrote up our project. (before)
   We visited the tomb *before writing up* our project.

2 We saw the crown jewels, then made our way to the exit. (After)
   _____, we made our way to the exit.

3 When he discovered the buried treasure the boy shouted out loud. (On)
   _____, the boy shouted out loud.

4 Meeting the famous historian was wonderful. (which)
   We met the famous historian, _____.

5 I wrote my history essay. I researched it first. (Before)
   _____, I researched it.

6 They broke the lock; they got into the castle. (By)
   _____ the lock, they got into the castle.

7 An expert claims to have found an Inca tomb. This has surprised everyone. (which)
   An expert claims to have found the tomb of an Inca king, _____.

8 After they had stolen the gold, the pirates sailed away. (Having)
   _____, the pirates sailed away.

4 **Find the mistake in each of these sentences and correct it.**

1 The palace where the Pharaoh lived it was very beautiful.
   The palace where the pharaoh lived was very beautiful.

2 That was the most interesting museum what I have ever seen.

3 His son, which was next in line to the throne, was murdered.

4 Archaeologists found the body they'd been looking for it.

5 In the book, was written recently, you can read all about the First World War.

6 I loved the castle you took me last year.

USE OF ENGLISH
Vocabulary: nouns from verbs and prepositions

1 Match the words (1–8) with their meanings (a–h).

1	downpour	**a**	An attempt by people in a country to change their government by force
2	upbringing	**b**	When something bad starts, such as a serious disease or a war
3	outcry	**c**	The final result of a meeting, process, etc.
4	turnaround	**d**	The money you receive regularly, e.g. from your work
5	uprising	**e**	The way your parents care for you and teach you as a child
6	outbreak	**f**	A complete change from a bad situation to a good one
7	income	**g**	An angry protest by a lot of people
8	outcome	**h**	A lot of rain that falls in a short time

2 Make these verbs into nouns ending in the preposition, *down*, *out* or *over*.

1 take + _____*over*_____ = a _____*takeover*_____
2 break + _____ = a _____
3 work + _____ = a _____
4 crack + _____ = a _____
5 hand + _____ = a _____
6 check + _____ = a _____
7 make + _____ = a _____
8 turn + _____ = a _____

3 Complete the sentences by adding a preposition to the verb to make a noun.

1 Have you got a copy of the _____*handout*_____ the lecturer gave us? (hand)
2 The police have had a _____ on the numbers of people who drink and drive. (crack)
3 Heavy storms turned the firework party into a complete _____. (wash)
4 There was a _____ on the motorway which caused big traffic jams. (break)
5 I'll wait at the _____ if you run and find the history book you want to buy. (check)
6 The archaeologists were disappointed at the poor _____ for their lecture. (turn)
7 If you're in a bad mood, go to the gym and have a good _____ – it'll make you feel much better! (work)
8 The museum has had a complete _____ and it looks really up to date now! (make)

4 Use the clues to complete the crossword.

Across
3 The parts of something that are left after the other parts have been destroyed
4 Magic words that bring someone bad luck
5 Belonging to a time in history that was thousands of years ago
6 All humans, considered as a group

Down
1 Someone who is related to a person who lived a long time ago
2 When rain stops something from happening, we say it is a _____.

USE OF ENGLISH
Grammar: cleft sentences; wh-clauses

1 **Rewrite the sentences starting with the words in brackets.**

1 I'm shocked at how the king behaved.
(What shocks)
What shocks me is how the king behaved.

2 My gran first got me interested in history.
(It was)

3 I'm surprised how long the inhabitants of the castle survived.
(What surprises)

4 During the tour we saw the queen's jewellery.
(What happened)

5 The prisoners were kept in a tiny underground jail.
(The place)

6 I'm interested in how little mankind really changes throughout its history.
(What interests me)

7 I really need some help with my project.
(What I really need)

8 The reason for the princes' deaths was a mystery.
(Why the princes died)

2 **Put the words in the correct order.**

1 with / the historian / didn't / I / said / agree / what / .
I didn't agree with what the historian said.

2 enjoy / what / you / you / are studying / Do / ?

3 hear / said / what / didn't / you / We / .

4 what / king / remember / did / can't / the / I / .

5 reason / because of / history / The / hate / is / I / the dates / .

6 horrified / tyrant / me / did / What / the / .

3 **Complete the article with one word in each space.**

The Inca civilisation

I've always been interested in the past, but 1) ____*it*____ was my Spanish teacher who got me interested in American history. The period I enjoy reading about most 2) _____ the time when the Incas ruled Peru. 3) _____ I admire most about their civilisation are the huge monuments and roads they built and the wonderful gold and silver works of art they created. But it is their final great leader, Atahualpa 4) _____ really appeals to my imagination. It was 5) _____ he was the Inca of this great empire that soldiers from Spain, the 'conquistadores' arrived. Their reason for coming to Peru 6) _____, of course, to steal the gold and silver and take it back to Spain. I have never understood 7) _____ Atahualpa agreed to meet the soldiers, but he did. And it was this act of trust 8) _____ led to his death, when the Spanish soldiers broke their promise, killed him, and then attacked and robbed his people. A sad end for a wonderful civilisation.

4 **Rewrite the sentences using the words in capitals. Use between two and five words, including the word given.**

1 My teacher gave me a love of history.
IT
It was my teacher who gave me a love of history.

2 I love exploring the past.
WHAT
_____ exploring the past.

3 She didn't listen to my words.
SAID
She didn't listen to _____.

4 We need more information before we start.
IS
What _____ more information before we start.

5 We love going to museums.
WE
Going to museums _____.

6 Nobody knows the place it happened.
WHERE
_____ is a mystery.

LISTENING

1 🔊 **10.1 Listen to a presentation about famous outlaws and choose the correct answers. Sometimes there is more than one correct answer.**

1 Jesse James had fought on *the losing/ the winning/neither* side during the American Civil War.

2 Jesse formed a gang with *his brother/ some outlaws/some soldiers.*

3 The James gang robbed *trains/houses/ banks.*

4 Jesse was shot by someone from *his family/the gang/the local people.*

5 Bonnie married at the age of *fifteen/ sixteen/seventeen.*

6 Bonnie fell in love with Clyde, who then spent some time in *Mexico/college/ prison.*

7 During their life of crime, the couple sometimes *murdered/robbed/ kidnapped* policemen for fun.

8 In the end, the couple were *shot/ hanged/stabbed.*

2 🔊 **10.2 Listen again and complete the sentences (1–10) using one word or a number from the presentation.**

1 Jesse James came from a _____*state*_____ in the USA called Missouri.

2 Jesse James fought in the American _____ War.

3 The James gang carried out their crimes in the American Wild _____ .

4 A judge offered a _____ to anyone who would bring Jesse James to him.

5 Jesse met his death at the age of _____ .

6 Bonnie liked writing _____ .

7 She first married when she was _____ .

8 Clyde was a very good _____ so the police couldn't catch up with him.

9 The couple slept in their _____ .

10 Bonnie and Clyde killed a total of _____ people.

SPEAKING SKILLS

1 Put the words in the correct order.

1 been / It / have / a / life! / hard / must
   It must have been a hard life!

2 to / It's / about history. / important / learn
   _____

3 I find / extremely / hard / to imagine / it / in the past. / life
   _____

4 do / like / about / I / local history. / learning
   _____

5 a / difference / big / two photos. / between these / There's
   _____

6 This / picture's quite / whereas the / a / other / recent / is / from / past / century.
   _____

7 learn / It's / about / to / world history. / fascinating
   _____

8 as interesting / that / This / one. / photo / as / isn't
   _____

2 Look at the photos opposite and complete the text with one word in each space.

1) _____*These*_____ photos show important events from history, 2) _____ the events are very different. This one was taken at ... I'm not sure how you 3) _____ it, a coronation? And the other is when the first men walked on the moon. Neither photo shows an event from 4) _____ history – they both took place last 5) _____ ! . I 6) _____ think studying history is important. We need to learn from past mistakes if we're going to avoid fighting and wars in the future. That's an 7) _____ important reason to study history, 8) _____ it?

WRITING

1 Which *three* of the following are usually found in an article?

   a formal language   **d** bullet points

   b an introduction   **e** interesting vocabulary

   c rhetorical questions

2 Article writers usually do these three things. Put them in the correct order (1–3).

   a Provide an interesting conclusion

   b Establish the topic and engage the reader

   c Give detailed information about the topic

3 Read the task. Then answer the question about it.

> You see this announcement on a history website.
>
> **Articles wanted!**
>
> **A great place to learn about history!**
> Where do you like learning about the past? Is it a museum, a castle, an old historic house, or the old part of a city? Why is this a good place to go?
>
> Send us your articles, and we will publish the best one on our website.

Which of these introductions, A or B, is the more interesting one?

A People often say that history is boring, but it's not – have you ever been to Aster Castle? It's the most fascinating place, and this is why.

B It's nice to learn about history and you can go to Aster Castle – it's very old.

4 This is part of the main section of the article. Choose the best words to make it interesting.

> There is a 1) *fascinating* / *big* library with so many old books – that sounds 2) *very* / *incredibly* boring, but in fact they are full of 3) *wonderful* / *square* pictures. The rooms are beautiful, and you can walk around them for hours looking at the paintings on the walls and 4) *thinking* / *imagining* what life was like then. It's a 5) *magical* / *nice* place.

5 Choose the best sentence to finish the article.

   A In fact, I like Aster Castle.

   B All in all, Aster Castle is a great place to learn about history!

6 Write your own answer to the task in 140–190 words.

Revision Unit 10

1 Complete the sentences with these words.

> buried   century   ~~death~~   descendant
> outbreak   rehearsal   tyrant   war

1 On the _death_ of Queen Elizabeth, Prince Charles will become king in the UK.
2 John F Kennedy was president of the USA during part of the twentieth _____ .
3 At the moment I'm reading about the Second World _____ .
4 After they die, do you know where most of the kings and queens of England are _____ ?
5 Adolf Hitler was a _____ who used his power in such a cruel and unjust way that he caused a war.
6 Prince William is a _____ of Queen Victoria who reigned over the United Kingdom in the nineteenth century.
7 There was a _____ on the day before the royal wedding so the prince and his bride could practise for the big day.
8 Many of the soldiers died due to an _____ of malaria.

2 Choose the best answer, A, B or C.

1 Official _____ of all historic events in our village are kept in the local government office.
   A records   **B** memories   **C** remembrances
2 The soldier was buried in a simple, unmarked _____ .
   A hole   **B** grave   **C** tomb
3 In 1692, Columbus set out on a long _____ which would take him to America.
   A expedition   **B** exploration   **C** discovery
4 Sending a man to the moon was one of the most fantastic achievements in the history of _____ .
   A persons   **B** mankind   **C** people
5 We're studying the history of _____ Greece.
   A ancient   **B** aged   **C** elderly
6 They've just unearthed the _____ of a dinosaur!
   A lasts   **B** rests   **C** remains

3 Complete the sentences with the correct form of the words in capitals.

1 She had a bad _upbringing_ .
   BRING
2 Have they completed the _____ of the Iron Age site?
   EXCAVATE
3 Centuries ago, rulers were often _____ to their victims.
   MERCY
4 We were _____ to hear of the death of the old king.
   SAD
5 The lecture was late starting because of a _____ on the motorway.
   BREAK
6 My friend, Clive claims to be the _____ of a Russian prince!
   DESCEND
7 The Borgias were _____ rulers who robbed and poisoned their people.
   FAMOUS
8 Have you seen the new _____ of Prince William and Kate? It's very lifelike.
   PORTRAY

4 Complete the words in the sentences.

1 The Pharaoh was buried in a magnificent t_o_m_b.
2 The victim's body was so badly m__t_____d that nobody could recognise him.
3 Nobody can agree on the causes of the war – they are very c_____e__t_____us.
4 As the film reached its climax, the audience's excitement grew to f__v__r pitch.
5 Two boys st_____b_____d upon the remains of the dinosaur as they were playing.
6 Claims about the d__s_____y of an Inca grave are being treated with suspicion.
7 Have you got the h__d_____t the teacher gave us in our last history class?
8 It was a snowy evening, so the t_____n_____t for the lecture was very low.

5 Complete the sentences with one word only.

1 Do you know the date _____*when*_____ war broke out?

2 We saw the castle _____ was destroyed in the rebellion.

3 _____ entering the tomb, the archaeologists found the prince's body.

4 Richard was the king _____ nephews were taken to the Tower.

5 Do you know _____ painted that portrait?

6 What surprises historians _____ that they found the grave so quickly.

7 Dad showed me the place _____ the battle took place.

8 _____ happened to the lost jewels is a mystery.

6 Join the sentences using the relative pronoun in brackets. Use commas only where necessary.

1 The monument is now a tourist site. The Incas built it. (which)
    The monument which the Incas built is now a tourist site.

2 The king reigned for forty years. His brother tried to kill him. (whose)

3 I know a museum. You can see amazing treasures there. (where)

4 Mr Stone is taking us on the history trip. He's a wonderful teacher. (who)

5 I can't remember the date. John F Kennedy died then. (when)

6 Have you read the news report? It claims they have found an Inca tomb. (which)

7 Complete the article with one word in each space.

8 Rewrite the sentences, using a relative/participle clause.

1 The prince was scared. He rode into battle.
    In spite of *being scared* , the prince rode into battle.

2 Frank didn't realise the object was so ancient. He picked it up in his hands.
    Not _____, Frank picked the object up in his hands.

3 Clare unearthed the gold coins. She shouted in surprise.
    After _____, Clare shouted in surprise.

4 First they finished their research; then they had a coffee.
    They finished their research before _____ .

5 Mum had never seen an Egyptian mummy before. She screamed in surprise.
    Never _____, Mum screamed in surprise.

6 We got off the coach. We stared up at the cathedral.
    On _____, we stared up at the cathedral.

7 Emma fell while she was getting off the coach.
    While _____, Emma fell.

8 David didn't speak as he led the way to the castle.
    Without _____, David led the way to the castle.

The **Real** Pirates

These days pirates are often cartoon figures or amusing characters in films like *Pirates of the Caribbean*. But 1) ____*what*____ we know from history books is that real life pirates were actually very violent. Francois L'Olonnais, 2) _____ was French by nationality, was one of the most infamous. He'd been attacked and nearly killed by Spaniards early on, 3) _____ gave him a lifelong hatred of Spain. He made this clear when, 4) _____ capturing a Spanish ship, he cut off the heads of all its sailors! L'Olonnais did not sail alone. As well as the ship 5) _____ which he travelled, he had seven other ships. He also led hundreds of men, with 6) _____ he terrorised the coast of South America. What he wanted 7) _____ the gold which treasure ships were carrying back to Spain. Many pirates had similar ambitions. However, the 8) _____ why we remember L'Ollonais is because he was merciless; he even ate the heart of a victim to make his friends lead him to hidden treasure. Forget the romance – pirates were some of the cruellest criminals in history!

READING

1 **Read the article and choose the correct answer, true or false.**

1 Young people find it difficult to avoid advertising.
   <u>True</u>   False

2 Advertising is forbidden in most schools.
   True   False

3 Marketers take advantage of teenage problems or difficulties.
   True   False

4 Product placement is a traditional form of advertising.
   True   False

5 Computer games often include product placement.
   True   False

6 Some advertising techniques could have a bad effect on society.
   True   False

2 **Read the article again. Choose which sentence (a–g) fits each space (1–6) in the text. You do not need one of the sentences.**

a They'll have made sure he uses a particular make or brand of these things all the time.

b The psychology behind this is very clever because you're so busy watching or playing you don't realise what's happening.

c Advertising appears in many forms and in many places.

d They're to be found everywhere on YouTube.

e Not only does it increase peer pressure among friends, it isolates any individual who either can't afford the product, or doesn't want it.

f Companies know that many young people have more spending power than ever before so they try to commercialise every possible aspect of their lives.

g These are just the kind of hang-ups that advertisers want to exploit.

YOU are the target!

Are you a teenager? If you are, you'll know how frequently advertisers target this age group and how difficult it is to escape their reach. 1) _f_ But what kind of impact is this having on such individuals – and on society as a whole? It's time to take stock.

2) _____ Brands and their logos are everywhere these days – particularly on the Internet where pop-up advertisements abound, in videos, and on cell phones. You can't escape it in school either – branding often appears on drinks or snack machines or on equipment. In fact, companies often fund schools in the knowledge that it will bring them good publicity and enable them to promote their products.

Advertisers know just how to target teenagers. They know young people often feel insecure and they work on this. You may worry about your physical appearance, for example, or whether you fit in with the rest of the gang. 3) _____ 'Worried about your appearance?' they ask. 'Don't panic, here is the perfect cream or lotion to make you look great.' Or, 'Worried about looking cool? No problem, just buy this phone and your friends will be SO impressed.' Owning the right stuff, they want to persuade you, is the most important thing in the world.

Product placement is one of the most successful advertising techniques around at the moment. Not content with traditional forms of advertising such as commercial breaks, marketers now promote products and brands by integrating them into movies, soap operas, reality shows, or even computer games. 4) _____ If the product is shown often enough, you'll remember it though!

One of the aims of product placement is to make you link your personality – real or ideal – to a particular product or brand. Take the Bond films, for example, aimed mainly at boys and young men. Do you admire the character of James Bond? Would you like to be as smart or cool as he is? If so, advertisers hope you'll look carefully at the car he drives, the clothes he wears, and the gadgets he uses. 5) _____ Next time you shop for a gadget, or clothes – or if you're old enough, a car – that identification with Bond may tempt you to buy the brands he used in the movie.

Marketers also want you to feel that ownership of a brand puts you in a select group. But this type of consumerism can be very divisive. 6) _____ Dividing people up in this way is bad for the individual and could be disastrous for society.

VOCABULARY
Fashion and shopping

1 Choose the correct word.

1 You shouldn't always give in to peer *pressure/persuasion*.

2 I've just bought the *last/latest* trainers with my birthday money!

3 I was disappointed with the DVD I bought because it didn't *give/live* up to its promise!

4 If you take your phone back to the shop and explain what's wrong with it they'll give you a *receipt/refund*.

5 The shop assistant had a long line of *customers/consumers* waiting to pay for their items.

6 If Dan boasts about his trainers to you, just *neglect/ignore* him!

7 Who needs designer *tickets/labels*? I think the people who buy them are just stupid.

8 Kids often *pester/exploit* their parents to buy trendy gadgets.

2 Complete the sentences with these words.

> bargain   buzz   devious   ~~impressionable~~
> pester   status   tempt   trendsetter

1 Advertisers try to influence *impressionable* young people.

2 I love shopping – I get a real .... out of it!

3 My little sister always tries to .... my mum into buying her something when we're out.

4 Sam is a real .... – everyone copies what he wears and does.

5 Some kids want to have the latest gadget as a .... symbol.

6 Sometimes advertising can be unfair or even completely ....

7 The salesperson tried to .... us to buy something, but we wanted to save our money.

8 Wait until the sales are on in the shops and things are reduced in price – that's when you can find a real ....

3 Make adjectives from these words.

1 comfort   →   *comfortable*
2 patience   →   ....
3 attract   →   ....
4 mercy   →   ....
5 fashion   →   ....
6 help   →   ....
7 fortune   →   ....

4 Complete the sentences with the correct form of the word in capitals.

1 I didn't buy the jeans because they were tight and *uncomfortable* .   COMFORT

2 Ken sighed ....; Janet was late again!   PATIENT

3 I don't like the latest fashion trends; in fact some of the styles are really ....   ATTRACT

4 Red was the 'in' colour last year, but now it's really ....   FASHION

5 Sally wanted to buy trainers like mine, but ...., they were all sold out.   FORTUNATE

6 I complained about the shop assistant because she was so ....   HELP

7 You sometimes get a bit of pain and .... when you wear shoes for the first time.   COMFORT

8 Mrs France didn't notice her child's .... until she had paid for her shopping.   APPEAR

GRAMMAR
Wishes and regrets

1 Choose the correct answer.

1 I wish you *came/could come* to the party!

2 Sophie wishes she *wouldn't have bought/hadn't bought* that ring.

3 I wish you *were/would be* coming on holiday with us.

4 If only I *had/would have* more pocket money!

5 Glen regrets *to get/getting* that tattoo now.

6 I wish the sun *came out/would come out*, but it's still cloudy.

7 We wish we *didn't eat/hadn't eaten* so much last night.

8 I wish they *stopped/would stop* putting so many ads on TV.

2 Complete the sentences with these verbs and any other necessary words.

> drive   give   have to   let   spend
> stop   ~~tell~~   warn

1 She regrets ___*telling*___ Paul her secret.

2 I haven't got any pocket money left. I wish I _____ it all!

3 James wishes he _____ his dad's car, but he's not allowed to.

4 Ella regrets _____ her phone number to Alan.

5 If only I _____ to attend school every day! I'd much rather stay at home.

6 Do you regret _____ Simon use your phone?

7 If only the teacher _____ us that we were having a test!

8 I can't get to sleep because my brother's in the next bed. If only he _____ snoring!

3 Complete the sentences using the words in brackets in the correct form.

1 I wish you ___*would listen*___ (listen) to me! You haven't heard a word I've said!

2 I wish I _____ (not/have to) leave now!

3 Gemma regrets _____ (promise) to meet Peter tonight.

4 I really miss you. I wish you _____ (sit) near me now!

5 Don't you wish you _____ (be) a bit older?

6 I wish I _____ (drive), but I'm too young.

4 Rewrite the sentences, using the word in capitals.

1 Mum is sad because she can't take a day off work.
SHE
Mum wishes ___*she could take*___ a day off work.

2 I'm sorry I bought this album now.
WISH
I _____ that album now.

3 Beth wishes she hadn't swapped her jacket.
SWAPPING
Beth _____ her jacket.

4 What a pity you didn't text me!
ONLY
If _____ me!

5 I'm sad you're not here.
YOU
I _____ here!

6 George is sorry he shouted at you.
REGRETS
George _____ at you.

7 I'm sad I'm not going shopping with you.
GO
I wish I _____ with you.

8 Amy is sad she's not sitting on a beach now.
WISHES
Amy _____ on a beach now.

USE OF ENGLISH
Vocabulary: intensifying adverbs

1 Find ten words on the topic of fashion and shopping. The words go across, down or diagonally. The first letter of each word is highlighted.

m	n	u	t	t	g	e	n	w	l	a	t	e	s	t
g	v	x	r	n	r	u	j	a	a	l	c	k	p	w
o	s	d	e	b	m	q	e	e	g	c	e	i	j	u
f	k	a	n	u	z	t	j	m	x	s	e	m	m	f
s	k	p	d	z	r	u	o	y	i	c	m	r	h	r
i	o	l	s	z	z	m	h	l	e	r	t	e	a	o
g	x	a	e	u	i	p	a	r	e	l	b	c	b	e
i	d	b	t	q	f	n	k	n	c	c	c	t	a	t
n	d	e	t	m	o	l	g	h	o	a	e	t	r	g
g	n	l	e	s	r	i	l	b	n	f	t	y	g	m
j	d	q	r	z	s	t	w	o	s	d	t	b	a	q
f	o	e	l	e	i	a	w	r	u	z	u	s	i	h
t	p	v	d	f	g	d	u	q	m	o	t	k	n	k
g	l	i	t	e	r	a	c	y	e	k	l	k	u	u
w	r	e	f	u	n	d	w	v	r	c	b	v	s	d

2 Choose the correct answer.

1 The fashion show was *absolutely/very* good.
2 I've been working *highly/incredibly* hard this morning.
3 That suit looks *very/absolutely* fantastic on you!
4 I was *bitterly/strongly* disappointed at the news.
5 My sister finds walking in such high heels *absolutely/very* impossible.
6 Their latest advertising campaign was *highly/strongly* successful.
7 We found making our own clothes *very/absolutely* difficult, but the end results were great!
8 I'm *utterly/bitterly* convinced I ordered the right size online.

3 Choose the correct answer, A, B, C or D.

1 My dad's _____ to his boss about improving the way they advertise the company.
  A asking   **B** discussing
  C talking   **D** interviewing
2 Beth _____ people's awareness of the environmental disaster by posting a clip on YouTube.
  A lifted   **B** raised
  C helped   **D** got
3 I had no _____ that advertisers filmed inside teenager's houses.
  A mind   **B** knowledge
  C though   **D** idea
4 I've had a lot of work to do recently, but I'm _____ near the end now.
  A going   **B** getting
  C reaching   **D** approaching
5 Our parents were _____ concerned about the amount of violence in the TV programme.
  A deeply   **B** utterly
  C bitterly   **D** absolutely
6 I haven't seen the advertisement you like, but I'll certainly _____ for it now.
  A look out   **B** put up
  C make up   **D** go in
7 I _____ ban advertisements on television if I had the choice!
  A could   **B** need
  C would   **D** ought
8 When my friend told me I could be a model, I never gave it a second _____.
  A mind   **B** thought
  C idea   **D** opinion

4 Complete the words in the sentences.

1 Something that's the most recent or the newest is called the l a t e s t.
2 If you are d ___ v _____ us, you use tricks or lies to get what you want.
3 Someone who is imp _____ ion _____ is easy to influence.
4 A tr _____ d is the latest fashion style.
5 If you t _____ t someone, you make them want to do something.
6 If you p _____ r someone, you ask them to do something many times.
7 Something you own that suggests you are rich or powerful is a s _____ s symbol.
8 Someone who buys or uses goods or services is a c _____ s _____ m _____ r.

USE OF ENGLISH
Grammar: *it's time, would rather*

1 Choose the correct answer.

1 It's time Alfie *cleaned*/*would clean* his shoes!
2 We'd rather *not to watch*/*not watch* that film tonight.
3 Hurry up! It's time *to go*/*we go*!
4 I *would*/*had* rather you didn't speak to me like that!
5 Isn't it time you *went*/*go* home?
6 Wendy would rather we *give*/*gave* her money for her birthday.
7 It's time you *got*/*would get* your hair cut!
8 I'd rather *play*/*playing* computer games than go shopping.

2 Complete the sentences with one word only.

1 I'd rather you _____were_____ my friend than my enemy!
2 I'd _____ Carla didn't borrow my things all the time.
3 I think it's _____ we went to bed.
4 It's time to _____ the TV off now.
5 I _____ rather have love than money!
6 Hurry up! It's time _____ leave.
7 I know you'd like to kiss me, but I'd rather _____ didn't!
8 We'd _____ leave the barbecue until next week, if that's OK?

3 Find the mistake in each of these sentences and correct it.

1 I'd rather you don't call me that!
   I'd rather you didn't call me that!
2 It's time Oscar goes home now!
3 I had rather you did not go out tonight.
4 We'd rather to walk than to drive.
5 Do you think it's time we take the cake out of the oven?
6 It's time I stop texting and do some homework, I'm afraid.

4 Complete the blog with one word in each space.

Advertisers are targeting teenagers ⇐ ➡

💬 View previous comments   Cancel Share Post

Advertisers are targeting teenagers more and more. So I think 1) _____it_____ is high time we protested about the tricks they use to make us buy things. They want us 2) _____ believe that buying a product will make us look trendier or more attractive. They 3) _____ rather we worried about how we look to our friends than considered whether we need a product or not. They'd also 4) _____ play on our fears of being left out than make us feel good. It's time 5) _____ fight back! Next time you see an advert online or on TV, ask 6) _____ some questions. Isn't it 7) _____ advertisers stopped interrupting our activities to exploit us in this way? Is it fair to use things like product placement and peer pressure so often 8) _____ we don't even realise how much we're being influenced. What do *you* think?

Write a comment   Support

LISTENING

1 Complete the collocations in the sentences using these verbs.

> broaden   follow   get   go   make
> put   ~~sort~~   spend

1 It's important to __sort__ out what's important and what isn't.
2 I often _____ mistakes, but that's how I learn.
3 I would never _____ against my parents' wishes and do something they really didn't like.
4 My teacher says I shouldn't worry when I _____ things wrong.
5 If you're unselfish you always _____ other people first.
6 A good teacher will _____ time helping their students.
7 Education is supposed to _____ students' minds.
8 A good role model provides an example for others to _____ .

2 🔊 **11.1 Listen to five teenagers talking about role models. Match these role models with the speakers (1–5). You do not need two of the words.**

> explorer   friend   ~~parent~~   politician
> singer   sportsperson   teacher

Speaker 1 _____ *parent*
Speaker 2 _____
Speaker 3 _____
Speaker 4 _____
Speaker 5 _____

3 🔊 **11.2 Listen again. Choose one thing that each speaker (1-5) has learnt from the list (a–h). You do not need three of the sentences.**

a Close friends are vital for a good life.
b I should never give up.
c Being patient is a useful quality in life.
d It's good not to be selfish.
e Success makes me happy.
f I should keep an open mind.
g It's important to have a good balance in life.
h How much money I earn is important.

Speaker 1 __*g*__
Speaker 2 _____
Speaker 3 _____
Speaker 4 _____
Speaker 5 _____

SPEAKING SKILLS

1 Match the sentences (1–5) with the follow-up sentences (a–e).

1 I often buy similar stuff to my mates.
2 I think adverts are a waste of time.
3 I always try to pay as little as possible.
4 I'd love to look like a film star.
5 I try not to ask my parents.

a They never know what young people like.
b They seem to have such a great life.
c We usually like the same things.
d I'll always look for a sale.
e I only remember the funny ones!

2 Read the question and match the sentences (1–5) in Exercise 1 with the five things (a–e).

> How much do you think these things influence young people when they are shopping?
> a discounts in shops __*3*__
> b opinions of friends _____
> c parents _____
> d advertising _____
> e articles about celebrities _____

3 Choose the correct words to complete the answers to the questions.

1   **A**   Are you influenced by celebrities?
   B   I enjoy reading about celebrities *but/and* I know I can never be like them and *so/because* I don't try to copy them.

2   **A**   Do you like shopping alone or with friends?
   B   I'd *rather/prefer* go shopping with friends, because I can ask them their opinion about things I'm thinking of buying.

3   **A**   Would you like to be rich and famous?
   B   I *wish/hope* I could be rich because then I could buy anything I wanted. But it won't happen. I think it's a *shame/regret* when people who are rich don't use their money to help other people. If only I could do that, I would *be/am* happy!

4   **A**   Do you think people buy too many things they want but don't really need?
   B   Yes, I do – and it's all because of advertising. It's a *pity/good* thing that there are so many advertisements everywhere – especially on the Internet! I hate those pop-up adverts – it's time they *were/are* banned!

WRITING

1 Read the pairs of phrases, (1–8), that are often used in opinion essays. Choose the more formal phrase, A or B.

1   **A**   I'm not sure that's completely true.
   B   I don't think that's right.

2   **A**   I guess most people think …
   B   I imagine the majority of people consider …

3   **A**   So, to conclude, I would say …
   B   So in the end, I think …

4   **A**   Whether this is a good or bad thing is another question.
   B   Is this good or bad? I haven't got a clue!

5   **A**   I think that …
   B   I personally feel that …

6   **A**   As you know, …
   B   It is a fact that …

7   **A**   It is thought that …
   B   People think that …

8   **A**   … but this is not completely accurate.
   B   … but this is rubbish.

2 Read the homework essay question and the sentences from a student's essay that answers it. Add a comma to each sentence.

> **Homework**
> Essay title
> Advertising to children under the age of sixteen should be banned. Do you agree?
>
> Write about
> 1 pester power
> 2 peer pressure
> 3 your own idea

1   Everywhere we look, advertisers direct their efforts to children.

2   Personally I feel that children under the age of sixteen should not be constantly subjected to advertising.

3   As they are very impressionable young children cannot possibly know what is good and what is bad for them.

4   If small children see things they want on television they will pester their parents for them.

5   This is not good for the children or indeed their parents.

6   In fact pressure from advertising can cause unnecessary arguments in the home.

7   While many people agree with this view others regard advertising as fairly harmless.

3 Write your answer to the essay question in 140–190 words, using an appropriate style.

Revision Unit 11

1 Choose the correct answer, A, B, C or D.

1 We were _____ disappointed with the laptops we bought.
2 These trainers were a half-price _____ in the sales!
3 Advertisers think all teenagers want to wear designer _____ .
4 Keep your _____ in case you want to return the jacket to the shop.
5 I felt _____ to buy a new sports bag but my friend stopped me.
6 That jacket looks _____ good on you!
7 My shoes are the _____ fashion – do you like them?
8 My dad's boss drives a Mercedes; it's a status _____ .

1	(A) bitterly	B	strongly	C	highly	D	absolutely
2	A cost	B	product	C	buzz	D	bargain
3	A posters	B	labels	C	tablets	D	marks
4	A refund	B	note	C	receipt	D	paper
5	A nagged	B	tempted	C	pestered	D	attracted
6	A absolutely	B	very	C	highly	D	strongly
7	A last	B	late	C	latest	D	newest
8	A style	B	trend	C	look	D	symbol

2 Complete the sentences with the correct form of the word in capitals.

1 I'll have to stand up – this chair is really _uncomfortable_ .
COMFORT
2 Teenagers are often quite _____ young people.
IMPRESS
3 Gemma's boyfriend is very _____ ; how did she find someone so good-looking?
ATTRACT
4 Mum's in hospital and she's in some _____ with her broken leg.
COMFORT
5 I'd like a pizza, but I haven't got any money, _____ .
FORTUNE
6 Ken is stylish, but his brother's clothes are so _____ !
FASHION
7 I'm coming! Don't be so _____ !
PATIENCE
8 I asked a man the way to the shop, but he was really
_____ .
HELP

3 Choose the correct word.

1 The _critically/bitterly_ acclaimed film won an Oscar.
2 I'm _utterly/incredibly_ convinced that there should be strict rules about advertising to children.
3 The time is passing _incredibly/highly_ slowly this morning!
4 Advertisers have been _deeply/highly_ successful at targeting teens.
5 My dad _bitterly/highly_ objects to paying such high prices for petrol.
6 What you just told me is _strongly/absolutely_ absurd!
7 The advertising campaign was _strongly/highly_ successful.
8 These days the cost of living is _utterly/ridiculously_ high.

4 Complete the definitions. The first and last letters are given.

1 An adjective to describe someone who uses tricks or lies to get what they want is
d _e v i o u_ s.
2 A verb that means _to make someone want to do something_ is t_____t.
3 Someone who buys or uses goods or services is a c_____r.
4 The latest fashion style is called a t_____d.
5 A verb that means to _decorate something in your own way to show it belongs to you_ is
p_____e.
6 The money you're given back in a shop if what you've bought is not satisfactory is a r_____d.
7 Someone who is a leader of fashion is a t_____r.
8 The piece of paper that shows you have paid for something is a r_____t.

5 Find the mistakes in the sentences and correct them.

1 It's time we go.
   It's time we went.

2 I wish you are here!

3 She regrets to taking the sweets without paying for them.

4 I'd rather not to see that film.

5 I wish you didn't play that music – it's awful!

6 It's time we leave for the party!

7 Oh no, I'm late! If only the bus came.

8 I'd rather Paul he didn't come with us.

6 Complete the sentences with one word.

1 I wish you   *were*   here.
2 If only we _____ afford a holiday!
3 I think it's _____ we went to bed.
4 I really _____ arguing with Stella; it was stupid of me.
5 Hurry up! It's time _____ leave!
6 I'd rather _____ didn't tell Mum where I was last night!
7 I wish I _____ brought my umbrella.
8 Do you regret _____ so much money for that watch?

7 Complete the article with one word in each space.

8 Use the clues to complete the crossword.

Across

2 If something lives up to its _____, it is as good as people said it would be.

4 When you look at things in shops without intending to buy them

5 A strong feeling that you must do the same things as other people of your age if you want them to like you.

6 A feeling of excitement

7 To make someone do something by explaining why it is a good idea

Down

1 Clothes made by a famous fashion designer

3 To annoy someone by asking them to do something many times

Teen opinion This Week: Advertising!

For our teen opinion page this week, we thought it 1) ___*was*___ time we conducted a teen survey on advertising. Here's a summary of your ideas. It seems most of you enjoy watching adverts if they're funny and well-made but you wish advertisers would 2) _____ people choose when to watch them. '3) _____ only they'd stop interrupting our favourite TV shows!' was a typical comment in the survey.
It seems you don't trust brands either, so in future advertisers may regret 4) _____ so much money putting recognisable designs on their products. It seems you'd 5) _____ not be left behind if your friends have certain products, but the picture is confusing here. 'Sometimes I wish I 6) _____ stand out more and be different, but other times I just want 7) _____ fit in' was a typical comment here. Most of you have no income except pocket money, and you wish advertisers 8) _____ remember that and realise you are looking for products that are good value and reflect your personality.

Survey
Questionnaire

READING

1 Match (1–9) with (a–i) to make phrases.

1 take   a with the consequences of an action
2 have   b your identity by doing something
3 give   c a risk
4 live   d an example of something
5 put forward   e up someone's confidence
6 push   f an argument in favour of something
7 establish   g regrets about doing something
8 build   h expectations about something
9 fall short of   i boundaries and limits to extend themselves

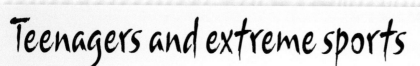

Teenagers and extreme sports

Living with teenagers who choose to take part in extreme activities such as solo sailing or paragliding can be challenging for their family. 1) __b__ Reconciling these two aims is not as easy as it sounds. Parents probably know that given the chance, teenagers are quite likely to go skiing off piste, possibly at great speed and without protective gear – it's all part of the fun. For teenagers, staying safe can appear boring.

One argument enthusiasts put forward in support of extreme sports compared with more mainstream ones is this. 2) _____ They give the well-known examples of the damage that can be done to young knees through powerful tackles in games of soccer, or to shoulder ligaments through the repetitive movements required in tennis. However, while the dangers of taking part in some extreme sports may be less precisely recorded, they are clearly present and it's only when something goes wrong that they become crystal clear. Extreme sports can never be completely safe and the only way for people to identify what the specific risks are is to keep doing them. Then if something goes wrong, anyone who gets injured has to live with the consequences – there can be no regrets.

Teenagers are able to do well in extreme sports on a physical level, although they could be unprepared in other ways, such as psychological. 3) _____ . This is because on these occasions they want to push boundaries. They won't necessarily choose to stop before managing to be the fastest going through white water rapids, or sailing further than anyone else, even if it's potentially dangerous. One young rock climber described the thrill of going out of his comfort zone, even though he was frightened. For many young people, that's what it's all about.

Is this attitude just the exuberance of youth, or is it down to something else, such as gender? 4) _____ It's not totally clear why they believe this as it's not true of all sports, or of all boys and girls; there are teenage girls who sail round the world, although it often seems to be boys who want to climb Everest. The answer may be that although they remain prepared to take risks, girls are more aware of the dangers and more open to the idea of doing something to reduce them if they can. 5) _____

Psychologists say that seeking out thrills and spills is part of growing up, and for many teenagers this is invaluable. If a teenager does well in a difficult situation it turns into a positive experience, and successful young round-the-world sailors would agree with that. 6) _____ If that happens, should parents continue to support their downhearted teenager in continuing with their extreme sport and build up their lost confidence, or should they try to steer them into safer activities? It's not an easy decision for either side to make.

2 **Read the article quickly and choose the best title.**

A The best sport in the world

B How to learn to do extreme sports

C Assessing the dangers of extreme sports

3 **Choose which sentence (a–g) fits each space (1–6) in the article. You do not need one of the sentences.**

a One result of this may be that they are unable or unwilling to think things through or make the right decision in some situations.

b All parents want their teenager to flourish and be happy, but at the same time they want him or her to stay safe.

c It's the responsibility of people organising extreme sporting activities to keep participants safe.

d Doing any kind of sport is risky in one way or another.

e However, the dilemma comes when they don't do well, or fall short of expectations.

f Some people suggest that boys may be willing to take more physical chances than girls.

g For example, one girl says that though she gets an adrenaline rush from snowboarding, she always wears a helmet and protective clothing.

VOCABULARY
Holidays and adventure

1 **Label the activities in the pictures.**

2 Choose the correct answer, A, B or C.

1 Some extreme sports involve putting your life
_____ risk.
  A in   **B** over   **C** at

2 White water rafting gave me a real
adrenaline _____.
  A hurry   **B** speed   **C** rush

3 For our geography trip, we're going on an
overland _____!
  A voyage   **B** expedition   **C** travel

4 Crossing the desert in such hot temperatures
was a real _____.
  A challenge   **B** attempt   **C** contest

5 Our hotel was off the beaten _____.
  A way   **B** track   **C** road

6 I'm glad my parents don't try to _____ me in
cotton wool.
  A capture   **B** tie   **C** wrap

7 I'd like to be a wildlife presenter and follow in
David Attenborough's _____.
  A footsteps   **B** footmarks   **C** footprints

8 I'd like a holiday in a really exotic _____.
  A station   **B** destination   **C** stop

3 Complete the sentences with the correct preposition.

1 Going _____*on*_____ an expedition must be
great fun.

2 My parents frowned _____ the idea of
us going on holiday alone.

3 We took part _____ all the activities.

4 I had to run to keep _____ with
my friends.

5 I'd like to try my hand _____ skiing.

6 Ralph wasn't allowed to go _____
the trip.

7 Our campsite was _____ the
beaten track.

4 Complete the words in the sentences.

1 You wear g _*o*_ g _*g*_ l _*e*_ s to protect your eyes
when you're diving.

2 We stopped to admire the qu _____ t, little
houses in the village.

3 My parents made me look at lots of
an _____ nt monuments.

4 Spain is my favourite holiday
des _____ a _____ on.

5 My sister wants to go on a solo v _____ e
round the world in her own boat.

6 I like holidays that set you some kind of
ch _____ ll _____.

5 Choose the correct word.

1 Zac broke the world *challenge/record.*

2 The village was very pretty and had lots of
white-washed/sandy cottages.

3 We saw plenty of *aged/ancient* monuments.

4 The hotel was on a long, *bending/winding* road.

5 Our summer holiday was packed with *non-stop/
up-down* excitement.

6 The people were very *hospitable/scenic.*

7 We saw photos of *quaint/sun-kissed* beaches.

8 Let me see those *break/holiday* brochures!

6 Find ten words on the topic of holidays and adventure. The words go across, down or diagonally. The first letter of each word is highlighted.

u	t	r	e	k	k	i	n	g	e	u	t	u	f	z
v	w	p	z	h	t	e	k	h	m	a	l	o	b	y
k	t	m	x	s	w	c	q	t	p	y	p	n	s	n
f	n	b	r	v	i	e	w	s	y	a	g	c	x	p
n	b	n	i	r	f	t	m	r	n	i	p	n	p	z
n	l	m	s	n	s	c	u	w	z	v	o	k	c	j
x	f	w	k	g	z	u	z	j	e	i	z	z	h	t
t	b	m	o	z	l	w	m	q	t	g	e	e	a	c
p	a	r	a	g	l	i	d	i	n	g	g	z	l	v
s	h	b	r	x	s	b	d	i	a	g	o	j	l	k
c	b	r	r	i	t	e	p	y	t	f	x	h	e	l
e	s	b	m	e	p	m	o	q	c	e	s	y	n	i
n	n	t	g	x	a	v	c	o	p	p	b	s	g	w
i	p	v	e	c	r	k	f	f	p	u	k	y	e	o
c	w	h	a	s	b	o	c	r	w	o	m	y	n	b

GRAMMAR
Modal verbs for degrees of certainty

1 Choose the correct answer, A, B or C.

1 The house is empty, so Mum _____ out.
  A must go
  B must have gone
  C must be going

2 Your dad _____ very happy when you broke your surfboard.
  A can't be
  B can't feel
  C can't have been

3 Tom's hands _____ when he dived from such a high rock.
  A must have been shaking
  B can have been shaking
  C can have shaken

4 Rock climbing is hard, so it's possible you _____ some training.
  A can need
  B may need
  C must need

5 Clare _____ sailing or she wouldn't spend so much time on it.
  A can be loving
  B must have loved
  C must love

6 Alfie gave up kite-surfing a long time ago, so he _____ it much.
  A can't have enjoyed
  B mustn't be enjoying
  C may not be enjoying

7 Sam _____ the race, but I'm not sure.
  A must have won
  B might have won
  C can have won

8 Our safari guide _____ very carefully or he would have seen the tiger first!
  A can't look
  B can't be looking
  C can't have been looking

2 Complete the sentences using the prompts.

1 Our neighbours have won a free holiday! They / must / run round their house and cheering!
  They must be running round their house and cheering!

2 I'm worried Ella's not here yet. She / might / get lost!
  _____

3 Gran brought up my dad by herself. That can't / be easy.
  _____

4 Get off the telephone, Jack! All the time you're using it, someone / might / try / to telephone me.
  _____

5 My mobile's not in my pocket! Someone / must / steal it.
  _____

6 Look how many old postcards Finn has. He / must / collect /them for ages!
  _____

7 Robert hasn't come out of school yet; he may / get detention.
  _____

8 That car's crashed into the bus in front; the driver / can't / pay attention.
  _____

3 Rewrite the sentences using the words in capitals. Use between two and five words, including the word given.

1 It's not likely they had a good holiday because they look so depressed.
  ENJOYED
  They *can't have enjoyed* a good holiday because they look so depressed.

2 I'm not sure if Sally is going to Africa.
  MIGHT
  Sally _____ to Africa, but I'm not sure.

3 There's no postcard here from Mike, so my guess is he forgot to send one.
  MUST
  There's no postcard here from Mike, so he _____ to send one.

4 I think it's impossible that the ship was travelling so fast.
  HAVE
  The ship _____ so fast.

5 It's possible we'll go on safari, but it's not certain.
  MAY
  We _____, but it's not certain.

6 It's not possible the plane has left yet.
  CAN'T
  The plane _____ yet.

7 I don't believe you're serious!
  BE
  You _____ joking!

USE OF ENGLISH
Vocabulary: -ful, -y and compound adjectives

1 Complete the sentences with compound adjectives, using the words in brackets.

1 I write with my right hand, but I see you are _left-handed_. (left/hand)
2 Diane gave an _____ scream as the hang glider rose higher. (ear/split)
3 My skiing instructor is _____. (kind/heart)
4 I'm hungry and that pizza looks absolutely _____! (mouth/water)
5 If something goes wrong in an extreme sport, it can have _____ consequences. (far-reach)
6 I like people who don't criticise everything and are _____. (open/mind)

2 Complete the article with the correct form of the word in brackets.

💬 View previous comments   Cancel Share Post

Extreme danger!
Would you take part in an extreme sport if you were given the 1) _choice_ (choose)? I'd always wanted to try caving even though it sounded quite a 2) _____ (scare) thing to do. So when my friend Steve suggested we have a go, I said 'yes'. I didn't tell my parents because I knew what their 3) _____ (react) would be. 'It's too dangerous. You can't go', they'd warn me. So, although I felt 4) _____ (guilt) about it, I said nothing. Everything went well as we climbed down into the cave. It was a bit 5) _____ (smell) but the rock formations were really 6) _____ (impress)! And it was so 7) _____ (peace) down there! We went further and further underground and the hole we were in got narrower and narrower. Then we had a 8) _____ (dread) shock. The hole was too small for us to go on – and there was no room to turn round and go back. We were stuck in the cave!

Write a comment   Support

USE OF ENGLISH
Grammar: indefinite pronouns

1 Choose the correct answer.

1 I'm not going *nowhere/anywhere* for my holidays.
2 There's *someone/something* really scary about that castle!
3 My dad's been nearly *anywhere/everywhere* in America.
4 There was *anything/nothing* good about my last holiday!
5 Our usual hotel was booked up, so now we haven't got *anywhere/somewhere* to stay.
6 *Someone/Anyone* should tell those people to be less noisy!
7 I've looked *somewhere/everywhere* for my sunglasses, but I can't find them!
8 I went to the campsite to find you, but no one *was/wasn't* there.

2 Complete the sentences with *whoever*, *whatever*, *whenever*, or *wherever*.

1 I hope my friend Sam's having a good holiday, _wherever_ she is.
2 _____ shares a room with my brother will discover that he talks in his sleep.
3 Dad says I have to text him when our plane lands, _____ the time.
4 _____ I go camping, it always rains!
5 I can take _____ I like on our next trip, so I'm going to choose Carla.
6 _____ I go, my little sister follows me!
7 Are you tired? We can go back to the campsite _____ you like.
8 Don't forget to pack the sun cream, _____ you do!

3 Complete the text with one word in each space.

The Trouble with Oscar

I'm going on holiday with my crazy friend, Oscar next year. My parents say I 1) *must be* be mad. Why? Because 2) _____ Oscar and I are together, 3) _____ goes wrong. I'll give you an example. Last week, Oscar and I had 4) _____ to do, so we decided to hang out in the park. 5) _____ we looked, we could see guys doing fun things, like practising extreme bike tricks. Oscar has always wanted to try this, so he asked a boy, James, to lend him his bike. James can't 6) _____ been thinking straight, because he agreed! Everything was OK until Oscar got ambitious. He tried to jump onto a wall, missed — and he and the bike hit 7) _____ ground hard! Oscar was OK — but the bike wasn't. Luckily, one of the other guys came to help. I didn't get his name but 8) _____ he was, he was brilliant! He got out some tools and repaired the bike then and there. James will never speak to us again, though! So Oscar, you see, is trouble!

LISTENING

1 🔊 **12.1 Listen to eight different people talking. Match the conversations (1–8) with the topics (a–e).**

a travelling as a job _4_
b transport problems causing a change of plans _____
c an unpleasant journey _____
d advice about a driving test _____
e enjoyable holiday travel _____

2 🔊 **12.2 Listen again and choose the correct answer, A, B or C.**

1 You hear a transport announcement. What caused the travel problem?
   A the weather
   B an accident
   C an important ceremony

2 You hear two people talking about a future trip. What is the girl doing in the conversation?
   A blaming the boy
   B reassuring the boy
   C sympathising with the boy

3 You hear two people talking about getting to school today. How did the boy travel?
   A by car   **B** by bus   **C** by bike

4 You hear someone talking about their work. What is the person's job?
   A tour guide
   B coach driver
   C flight attendant

5 You hear two people talking about a recommendation. How does the woman feel about the man's reaction?
   A annoyed
   B apologetic
   C unconcerned

6 You hear a boy talking about a trip. How long will the whole trip take?
   A one year   **B** six months   **C** nine months

7 You hear two teenagers talking at an airport. What does the girl think is a problem?
   A a missing passport
   B some lost luggage
   C finding the pharmacy

8 You hear a driving instructor talking about a driving test. Which advice does she include?
   A avoid asking the instructor anything
   B practise driving around with a friend
   C have a confident attitude towards the test

SPEAKING SKILLS

1 **Look at the photos of theme park rides and choose the correct words to complete the sentences.**

1 *Every/Each* of the photos shows a scene at a theme park.
2 I think the ride in Photo 1 is scarier *that/than* in Photo 2.
3 The ride in Photo 2 wouldn't make you feel *much/as* sick and dizzy as the ride in Photo 1.
4 *While/However* the ride in Photo 1 might be dangerous, the ride in Photo 2 wouldn't be.
5 The ride in Photo 2 is full of unexpected shocks and surprises *although/whereas* the ride in Photo 1 is more about speed and sensation.
6 There are hidden ghosts and skeletons on the ride in Photo 2; *however/besides* the ride in Photo 1 is just about speed and sensation.

2 **Complete what a student says about the two photos with one word in each space.**

1) ___*Each*___ photo shows a different ride at a 2) _____ park, and both are scary for different reasons. 3) _____ the first photo, the people 4) _____ on a fast-moving ride 5) _____ turns people upside down as 6) _____ as round and round! That would make me 7) _____ a bit sick! 8) _____, the ride in the second photo is frightening for another reason. 9) _____ tries to shock and surprise you by suddenly showing you ghosts and skeletons. I think 10) _____ rides make people feel scared, but in the first 11) _____ the fear comes from speed and sensation 12) _____ in the second picture it comes from the shock.

WRITING

1 Choose the five statements about stories that are true.

1. A story should hold the reader's interest.
2. A story can include dialogue.
3. A story should include colourful and interesting vocabulary.
4. Stories often include headings and bullet points.
5. A story should use clear linking and sequencing words.
6. A story should have a clear narrative that a reader can follow easily.

2 Choose the correct words to complete the story.

It was dusk when we reached our destination in the forest. We decided to make camp *firstly/immediately*. I put up the tent *during/while* the others started a fire to cook a meal. *At first/instantly* it all went well, but suddenly there was a strong gust of wind and an ember from the fire was blown onto the tent. *Instantly/secondly* it burst into flames. Luckily none of us was near it at the time, but the problem was that *at the moment/now* we had nowhere to sleep. This was where my mobile phone came into its own! I contacted the local ranger, *that/who* came and took us to a lodge for the night.

3 Read the paragraph. Find and correct the six spelling mistakes.

I've always been keen on travalling, and I hope to be able to go round the world one day. I'd love to spend a year visitting places I've only seen on television, but first I have to save up enough money to do it. I'll have to make do with hollidays with the family for the moment, but as soon as I've saved enough I'll be off. I want adventure and excitment! Last holiday we did manege to trek to the top of a small mountain, but it was rather tame really. I did have to rescue my little sister who tripped and sprained her anckle – I had to carry her all the way down!

4 Read the task and complete the story using the sequencing expressions in the box. You do not need one of the expressions.

You have seen this announcement in an English language magazine for young people.

We need stories for our magazine! Your story must begin with this sentence:
When Kelly saw the email she knew something was wrong.
Your story must include:
• a map
• a rescue

Write your story in 140–190 words.

after   after a while   after that   suddenly
as soon as   ~~earlier~~   ever since   first   thirdly

When Kelly saw the email she knew something was wrong. Carol had gone walking in the mountains two days 1) _____earlier_____ , and had been keeping in touch through social media 2) _____ . The email from Carol's best friend said Carol's messages had suddenly stopped and there was no indication of where she was. Her mobile phone was dead.

Luckily Kelly knew the area well. She packed up her climbing and camping equipment ready to start out the following morning, because she knew there was no time to be lost. 3) _____ she arrived in the area, she began following the same route as Carol, using a map as a guide. Although the weather was terrible, Kelly's training and experience kept her safe. 4) _____ walking all day, she set up camp for the night. The moment it was light, she set off again, thinking that she must be getting near to Carol's last known position.

She was walking along a rocky ridge when 5) _____ she heard a weak shout of 'help'! It was coming from below the ridge. She scrambled down and saw Carol lying on the ground, with a broken leg. 6) _____ Kelly gave her water and made her comfortable, and 7) _____ she radioed for help. 8) _____ a helicopter arrived and took Carol to hospital.

5 Write your own answer to the task in 140–190 words, using an appropriate style.

Revision Unit 12

1 Choose the correct answer, A, B, C or D.

1 Your success in the sailing competition was really _____.
  - **A** attractive   **(B)** impressive
  - **C** interesting   **D** sensitive

2 Dad would never have booked such a terrible hotel if he'd been thinking _____.
  - **A** straight   **B** well
  - **C** right   **D** good

3 I tried to persuade my brother to lend me his new tent, but he was having _____ of it.
  - **A** nothing   **B** anything
  - **C** none   **D** something

4 I'd really love to try my _____ at kite surfing.
  - **A** arm   **B** foot
  - **C** head   **D** hand

5 Don't walk so quickly! I can't keep _____ with you!
  - **A** on   **B** off
  - **C** up   **D** in

6 Trekking through the jungle in that heat was a terrible _____.
  - **A** ordeal   **B** torture
  - **C** deal   **D** work

7 Our teacher _____ on the idea of sleeping under the stars; she insisted we slept in tents.
  - **A** refused   **B** frowned
  - **C** complained   **D** banned

8 His _____ to sail solo round the world ended in disaster.
  - **A** effort   **B** trial
  - **C** go   **D** attempt

2 Match an activity with a definition.

1 rowing
2 abseiling
3 canoeing
4 caving
5 diving
6 paragliding
7 surfboarding

a Standing on a plastic board so that you can ride the ocean waves
b Flying/gliding slowly through the air attached to a parachute shaped like a wing
c Going down a large, natural hole in the side of a hill, or under the ground
d Jumping into water with your head and arms first
e Making a small boat move across the water using long sticks called oars
f Paddling along in a long, narrow boat which is pointed at both ends
g Sliding down a rope and pushing against the wall or cliff with your feet

3 Complete the sentences with the correct form of the word in capitals.

1 I found hang-gliding a really _____scary_____ experience.   SCARE
2 The village we stayed in was a bit too _____ for me!   PEACE
3 Walking in the jungle made me all hot and _____.   SWEAT
4 The panoramic views from the top of the castle were extremely _____.   IMPRESS
5 After a while, we had to let some air into the tent because it was so _____.   STUFF
6 We complained because the air conditioning in our hotel room was _____.   FAULT
7 The walls of our hostel were painted with lovely, _____ designs.   COLOUR
8 Your _____ of holiday sounds great!   CHOOSE

4 Complete the sentences with compound adjectives formed from the words in brackets.

1 My friends all write with their right hands but I'm _left-handed_. (left/hand)
2 Marco comes from the south of Italy so he's quite _____. (dark/skin)
3 I wish my dad wasn't so _____. (short/temper)
4 If people are _____ (open/mind), they are willing to consider new ideas and opinions.
5 My grandad is so _____ (kind/heart) – he'd do anything for anyone!
6 I used to think sharks were _____ (cold/blood) killers, but I don't any more.
7 Pamela's decision to give up university had _____ (far/reach) consequences.
8 Our tour guide was tall, _____ (long/hair) and suntanned.

GOLD EXPERIENCE

5 **Find the mistakes in the sentences and correct them.**

1 Oh no! I must leave my aeroplane ticket in the car!
Oh no! I must have left my aeroplane ticket in the car!

2 I went to Paula's house, but nobody wasn't there.

3 Brian must not be staying all week – I'm not sure.

4 I've got anything to wear to the disco tonight.

5 It's only six o'clock. She mustn't have gone to bed yet!

6 Listen, anybody! I want you all to come to our party tonight.

7 I can't believe a word he's saying. He must tell lies!

8 She's been nearly anywhere in Europe except the United Kingdom.

6 **Rewrite the sentences using the word in capitals. Use between two and five words, including the word given.**

1 I was scared by the film.
REALLY
The film was *really scary* .

2 It's impossible that you booked the room because there's no record of it.
HAVE
You _____ booked the room because there's no record of it.

3 The house was empty when I called.
WAS
_____ at home when I called.

4 The room smelled extremely bad.
VERY
The room was _____ .

5 It's possible Gary is trying to phone you right now.
MIGHT
Gary _____ phone you right now.

6 I'm sure we're too late for the plane.
MISSED
We _____ the plane.

7 There's no noise outside.
VERY
It is _____ outside.

7 **Complete the sentences with a word beginning with *some-*, *any-*, *every-*, or *no-*.**

1 Has *anyone* seen Amanda? I think she's lost.

2 _____ has left their handbag on the coach!

3 We had no complaints about our holiday; _____ enjoyed it.

4 I phoned the holiday company, but there was _____ there to answer the phone.

5 Is there _____ at all I can do to help?

6 We've got to find _____ to stay overnight.

7 If you've missed the only flight, there's _____ anyone can do about it.

8 I've looked for my passport, but I can't find it _____ .

8 **Use the clues to complete the crossword.**

Across

1 An adjective used to describe a place or road which has beautiful views of the countryside

4 An adjective to describe food that looks and tastes really good

7 An adjective meaning *friendly and welcoming to visitors*

8 An adjective meaning *curving or bending many times*, usually used to describe a road or path

Down

2 An adjective which means *without stopping*

3 Something you probably don't want your parents to wrap you in

5 An adjective which is used to describe houses whose walls are painted white

6 An adjective which is used to describe a very loud, high scream

Exam information

The *Cambridge English: First for Schools* is made up of four papers, each testing a different area of ability in English. The Reading and Use of English Paper is worth 40 per cent of the marks (80 marks), and each of the other papers is worth 20 per cent (40 marks each). There are five grades. A, B and C are pass grades; D and E are fail grades.

Reading and Use of English (1 hour 15 minutes)

Part 1 Multiple-choice cloze	Focus	Vocabulary/Lexico grammatical
	Task	You read a text with eight gaps. You choose the best word or phrase to fit in each gap from a set of four options (A, B, C or D).
Part 2 Open cloze	Focus	Grammar/Lexico grammatical
	Task	You read a text with eight gaps. You have to think of the best word to fill each gap. No options are provided.
Part 3 Word formation	Focus	Vocabulary/Lexico grammatical
	Task	You read a text with eight gaps. You are given the stems of the missing words. You have to change each word to fit the context.
Part 4 Key word transformations	Focus	Grammar and vocabulary
	Task	There are six items. You are given a sentence and a 'key word'. You have to complete a second, gapped sentence using the key word. The second sentence has a different grammatical structure but must have a similar meaning to the original.
Part 5 Multiple-choice questions	Focus	Detail, opinion, attitude, text organisation features, tone, purpose, main idea, implication, meaning from context.
	Task	There are six four-option multiple-choice questions. You have to choose the correct option (A, B, C or D) based on the information in the text.
Part 6 Gapped text	Focus	Understanding text structure, cohesion, coherence
	Task	You read a text from which six sentences have been removed and placed in jumbled order after the text. There is one extra sentence that you do not need to use. You must decide from where in the text the sentences have been removed.
Part 7 Multiple matching	Focus	Specific information, detail, opinion and attitude
	Task	You read ten questions or statements and a text which has been divided into sections, or several short texts. You have to decide which section or text contains the information relating to each question or statement.

Writing (1 hour 20 minutes)

The Writing paper has two parts, and you have to complete one task from each part.		
Part 1	Focus	Outlining and discussing issues and opinions on a particular topic
	Task	Part 1 is compulsory, and there is no choice of questions. You have to write an essay based on a title and notes. You have to write 140–190 words.
Part 2	Focus	Writing a task for a particular purpose based on a specific topic, context and target reader.
	Task	Part 2 has four tasks to choose from which may include: • a letter or email • an article • a report • a review • an essay • a story. The fourth option is based on a set text. You have to write 140–190 words for Part 2.

Listening (approximately 40 minutes)

Part 1 **Extracts with multiple-choice questions**	*Focus*	Each extract will have a different focus, which could be: main point, detail, purpose or location of speech, relationship between the speakers, attitude or opinion of the speakers.
	Task	You hear eight short, unrelated extracts of about thirty seconds each. They may be monologues or conversations. You have to answer one three-option multiple-choice question (A, B or C) for each extract.
Part 2 **Sentence completion**	*Focus*	Specific information, detail, stated opinion
	Task	You hear a monologue or conversation lasting about three minutes. You complete ten sentences with words from the text.
Part 3 **Multiple matching**	*Focus*	Gist, detail, function, attitude, purpose, opinion
	Task	You hear a series of five monologues or exchanges, lasting about thirty seconds each. The speakers in each extract are different, but the situations or topics are all related to each other. You have to match each speaker to one of six statements or questions (A–F). There is one extra option that you do not need to use.
Part 4 **Multiple-choice questions**	*Focus*	Specific information, opinion, attitude, gist, main idea
	Task	You hear an interview or conversation which lasts about three minutes. There are seven questions. You have to choose the correct option (A, B or C).

Speaking skills (approximately 14 minutes)

You take the Speaking test with a partner. There are two examiners. One is the 'interlocutor', who speaks to you, and the other is the 'assessor', who just listens.

Part 1 **Interview** (3 minutes)	*Focus*	General interactional and social language
	Task	The interlocutor asks each of you questions about yourself, such as where you come from, what you do in your free time.
Part 2 **Individual long turn** (4 minutes)	*Focus*	Organising your ideas, comparing, describing, expressing opinions
	Task	The interlocutor gives you two photographs to compare, and to give a personal reaction to. You speak by yourself for about a minute while your partner listens. Then the interlocutor asks your partner a question related to the topic. Only a short answer is expected. You then change roles.
Part 3 **Collaborative task** (3 minutes)	*Focus*	Interacting with your partner, exchanging ideas, expressing and justifying opinions, agreeing and/or disagreeing, suggesting, speculating, evaluating, reaching a decision through negotiation
	Task	You are given a task to discuss together, based on a set of pictures. You should try to reach a conclusion together, but there is no right or wrong answer to the task, and you don't have to agree with each other. It is the interaction between you that is important.
Part 4 **Discussion** (4 minutes)	*Focus*	Expressing and justifying opinions, agreeing and disagreeing
	Task	The interlocutor asks you both general questions related to the topic of Part 3, and gives you the chance to give your opinions on other aspects of the same topic.

NOTES

NOTES

Pearson Education Limited
Edinburgh Gate
Harlow
Essex CM20 2JE
England
and Associated Companies throughout the world.

www.english.com/goldxp

First published 2016
Third impression 2018

ISBN: 9781292159492

Set in 10pt Mixage ITC Std
Printed by Neografia in Slovakia

Acknowledgements
The publishers would like to thank Jacky Newbrook and Lynda Edwards for their contributions to this new edition.
The publishers and author would like to thank the following people for their feedback and comments during the development of the material:

Elif Berk, Turkey; Alan Del Castillo Castellanos, Mexico; Dilek Kokler, Turkey; Trevor Lewis, The Netherlands; Nancy Ramirez, Mexico; Jacqueline Van Mil-Walker, The Netherlands

The publishers would like to thank the following for their kind permission to reproduce their photographs:

(Key: b-bottom; c-centre; l-left; r-right; t-top)

123RF.com: 4cr, 4b, 5tl, 5bl, 11, 67, Playalife2006 21br; **Alamy Images:** dpa picture alliance 90r, Andy Harmer 89, Image100 114, Ingram Publishing 21bl, INTERFOTO 90l, Yadid Levy 60t, NASA Images 101t, PhotoAlto sas 104, Pictorial Press Ltd 101b, sdbphoto.com 38, Kumar Sriskandan 63, Colin Underhill 60b; **Corbis:** Dean Pictures 52, Image Source 13, Matthias Kulka 29, Ocean 17, 69tr, 69br, PhotoAlto / Sigrid Olsson 8, The Gallery Collection / Howard Pyle 103; **Creatas:** 16cr; **Digital Vision:** 16br; **DK Images:** Sarah Ashun 76l, Andy Crawford 32bl, Rough Guides / Suzanne Porter 99; **Fotolia.com:** antiksu 32br, Tony Baggett 84r, Rafael Ben-Ari 14r, BlueOrange Studio 14cl, Richard Carey 16tl, Jakub Cejpek 115cl, Javier Cuadrado 19, Rocco D'Auria 115br, Gokychan 16cl, hotshotsworldwide 16tr, lightwavemedia 41b, Audrey Liverneaux 16bl, Irmina Mamot 115cr, mgkuijpers 16tc, Tyler Olson 40t, 69tl, Lida Salatian 115bl, Gina Sanders 32tl, Nikolai Sorokin 32cr, Subbotina Anna 4cl, 5tr, WavebreakmediaMicro 43, xmasbaby 120t, Yakobchukv Olena 4t, 5br; **Getty Images:** Mark S Cosslett 118, Jim Dyson 58, Thomas Grass 49, luismmolina 76r, svetikd 106, World Perspectives 28; **Imagemore Co., Ltd:** 47; Pearson Education Ltd: 35bc, Sophie Bluy 35b, 65, Studio 8 64b, 73; PhotoDisc: Karl Weatherly 119; **Rex Shutterstock:** 46, Jenny Goodall / Daily Mail 23, Mantyla 77, Quirky China News 9, Universal History Archive / Universal Images Group 96; **Shutterstock.com:** 3Dsculptor 31, Thomas Bethge 61, Mircea Bezergheanu 14cr, Tony Campbell 21cr, CandyBox Images 115tl, Olga Danylenko 21tr, Steve Davis 86, EpicStockMedia 115tr, Juergen Faelchle 24-25, Feature Flash Photo Agency 45, Iakov Filimonov 84l, gorillaimages 69bl, gregdx 120b, Hasloo Group Production Studio 66, Imageegami 64t, janprchal 80, Janelle Lugge 14l, Mai Techaphan 51, mangostock 41t, Pincasso 81t, Pixsooz 113, Andrey Popov 35t, Pressmaster 40b, Pruda 74, Repina Valeriya 53, Jose AS Reyes 95, Kazlouski Siarhei 81b, StockThings 98, Stuart Miles 111, Syda Productions 75, Gladskikh Tatiana 91, Denise Thompson 20, Vectomart 105, Wavebreakmedia 35tc, Jarno Gonzalez Zarraonandia 94; **Sozaijiten:** 32tr, 32cl; **SuperStock:** 59, Radius 37, Science Photo Library 33, Voisin / Phanie 83

Illustrated by: Caron Painter (Sylvie Poggio) 68; Andrew Painter 107, 109; Ned Woodman 92

Cover images: *Front:* **Shutterstock.com:** Alexander Yakovlev

All other images © Pearson Education

Every effort has been made to trace the copyright holders and we apologise in advance for any unintentional omissions. We would be pleased to insert the appropriate acknowledgement in any subsequent edition of this publication.